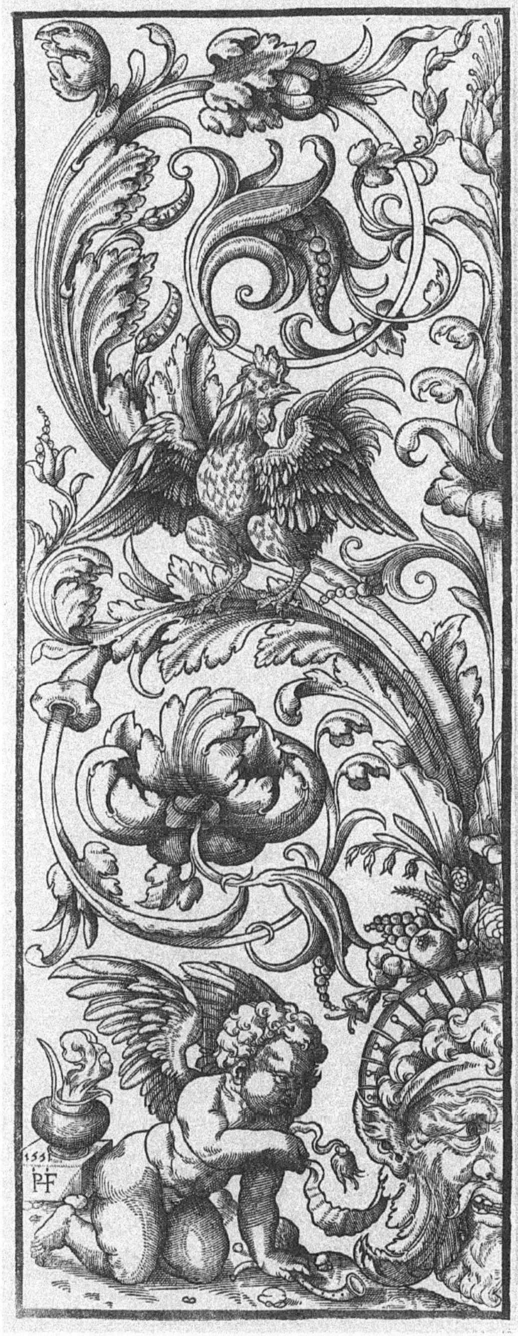

Fantastic Gothic & Renaissance Ornament

Edited by
Rudolf Berliner

Dover Publications, Inc.
Mineola, New York

Note

These richly detailed illustrations showcase Fantastic Gothic and Renaissance styles meticulously reproduced from a rare, early-twentieth-century portfolio. Imaginative figures, grotesque accents, gargoyles, griffons, and other mythical beasts intertwined with foliage, flowering stems, and swirls of vines adorn architectural elements and illuminated manuscripts in this exquisite treasury of ornament. Art historians and artists alike will enjoy this assortment of 127 unusual designs.

Bibliographical Note

This Dover edition, first published in 2008, is a new selection of plates from volumes I and II of *Ornamentale Vorlage-Blätter, Des 15. Bis 18. Jahrhunderts*, originally published by Klinkhardt & Biermann, Verlag, Leipzig, 1925.

DOVER *Pictorial Archive* SERIES

Library of Congress Cataloging-in-Publication Data

Berliner, Rudolf, 1886–
[Ornamentale Vorlageblätter des 15. bis 18. Jahrhunderts. Selections]
Fantastic Gothic and Renaissance ornament / edited by Rudolf Berliner.
p. cm. — (Dover pictorial archive series)
"This Dover edition, first published in 2008, is a new selection of plates from volumes I and II of Ornamentale Vorlage-Blätter des 15. bis 18. Jarhunderts, originally published by Klinkhardt & Biermann Verlag, Leipzig, 1925."
ISBN-13: 978-0-486-46017-8
ISBN-10: 0-486-46017-7
1. Decoration and ornament, Gothic—Catalogs. 2. Decoration and ornament, Renaissance—Catalogs. I. Title.

NK1530.B432 2008
745.4—dc22

2007041870

Printed in Canada
46017704 2025
www.doverpublications.com

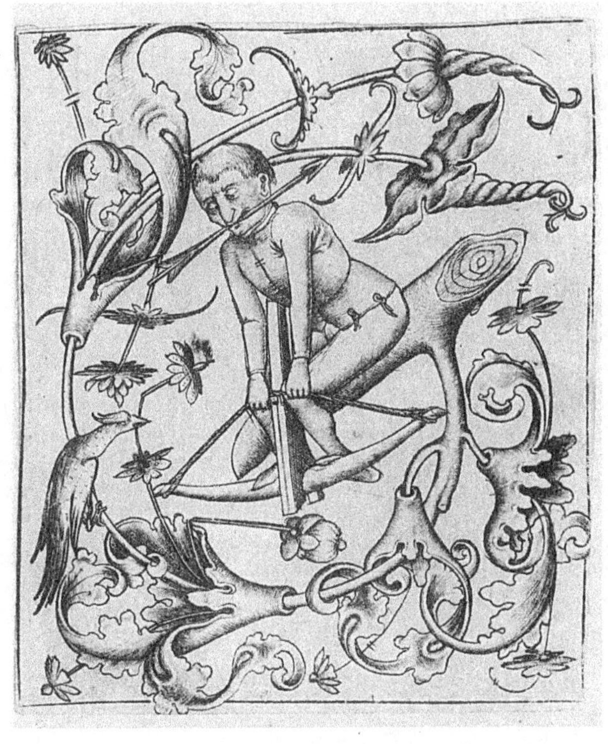

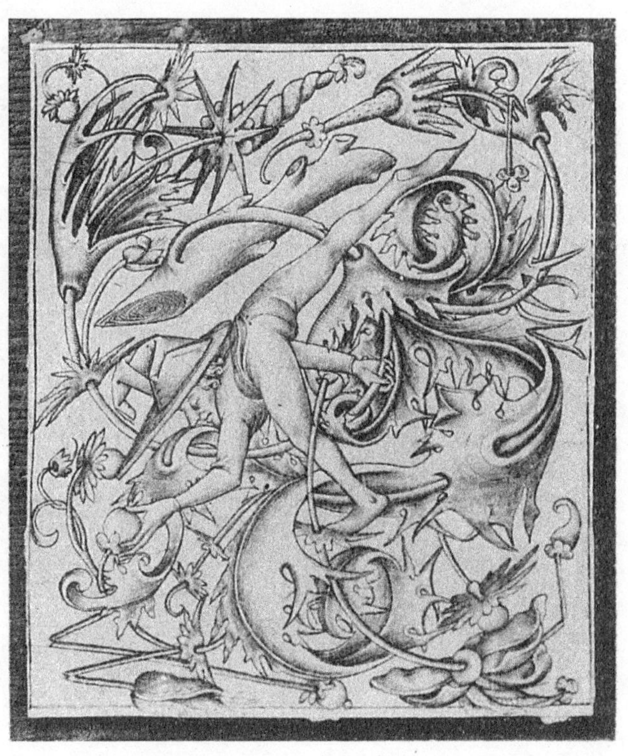

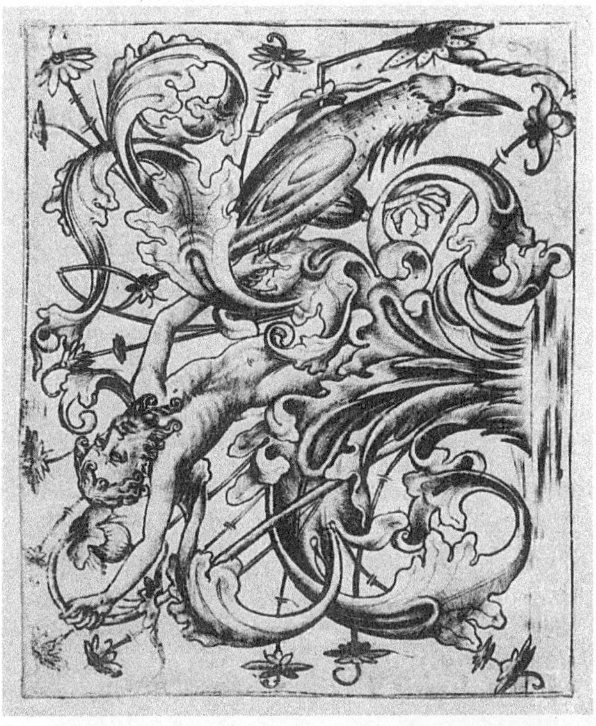

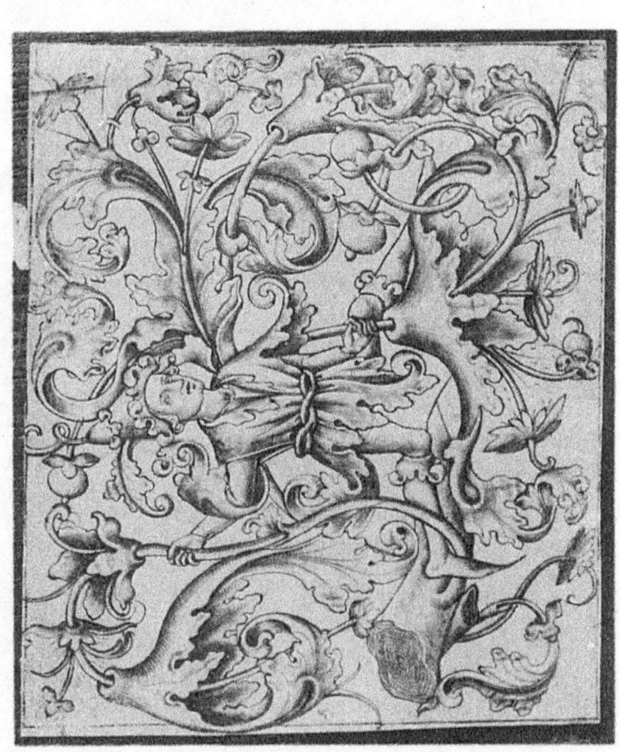

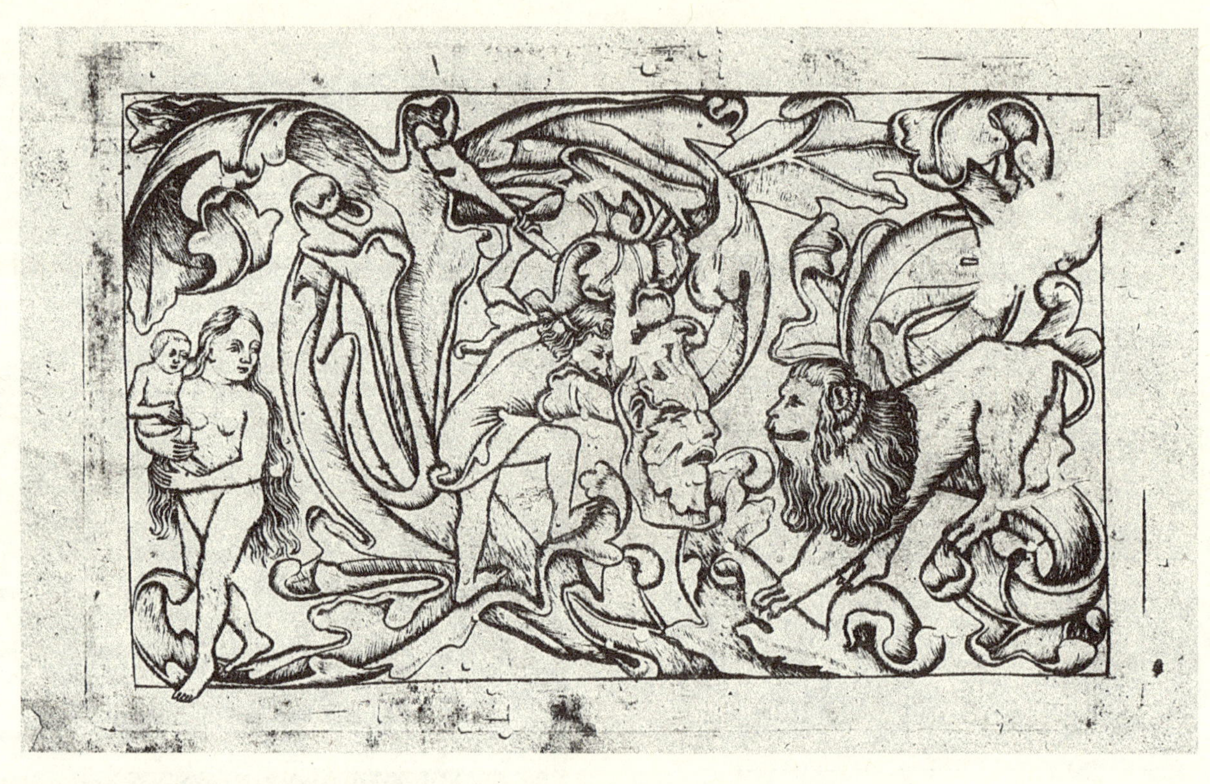

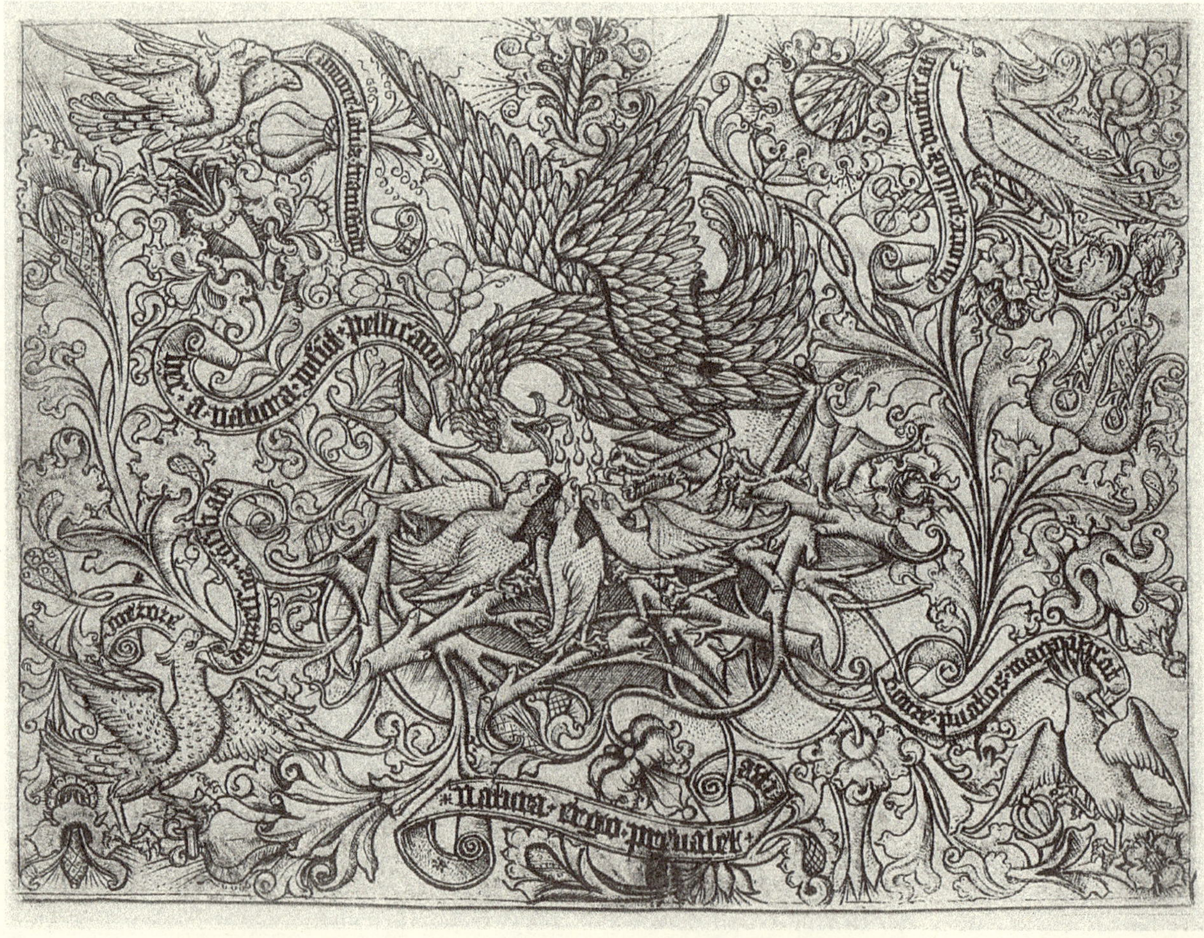

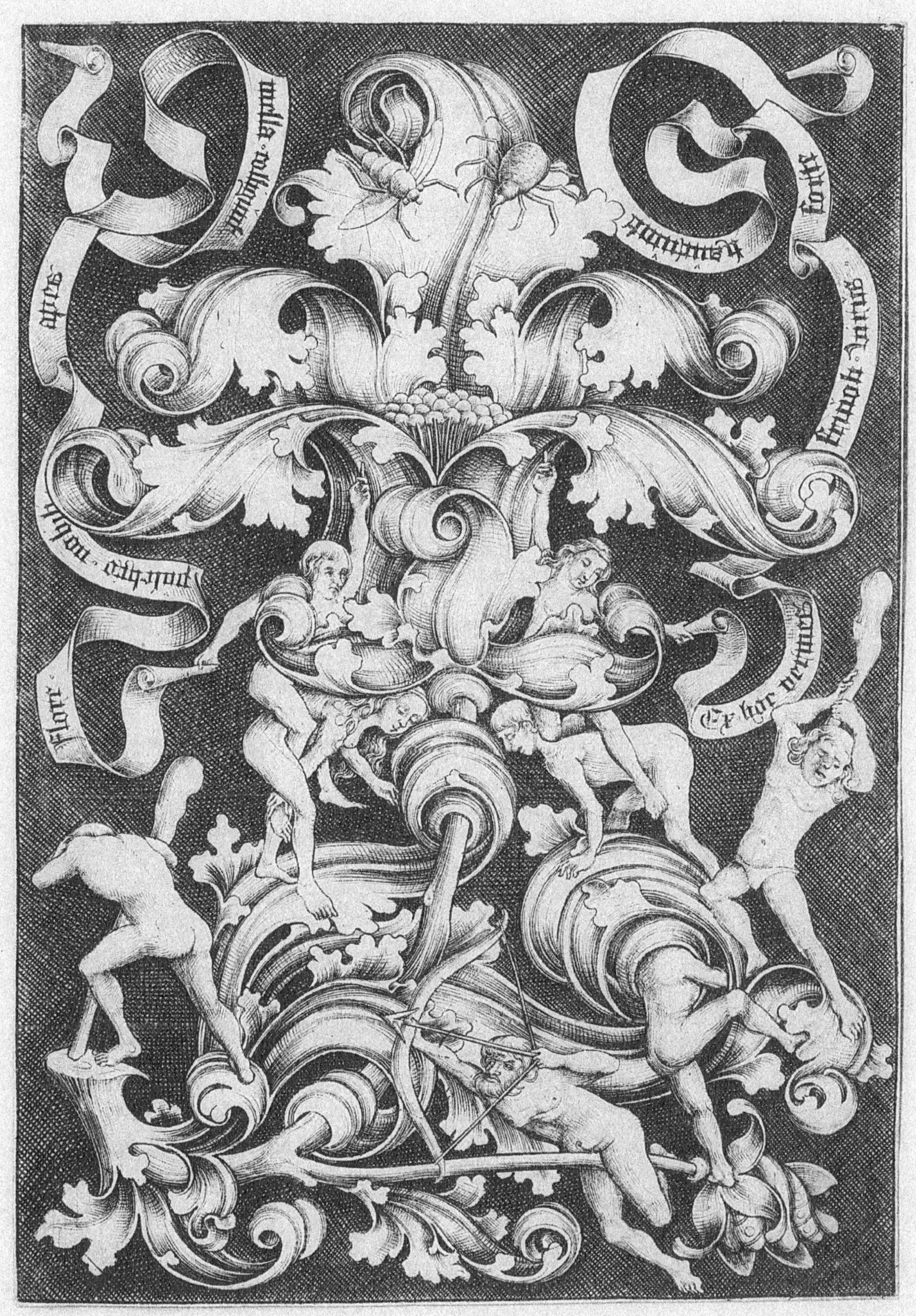
Ex hoc venimus

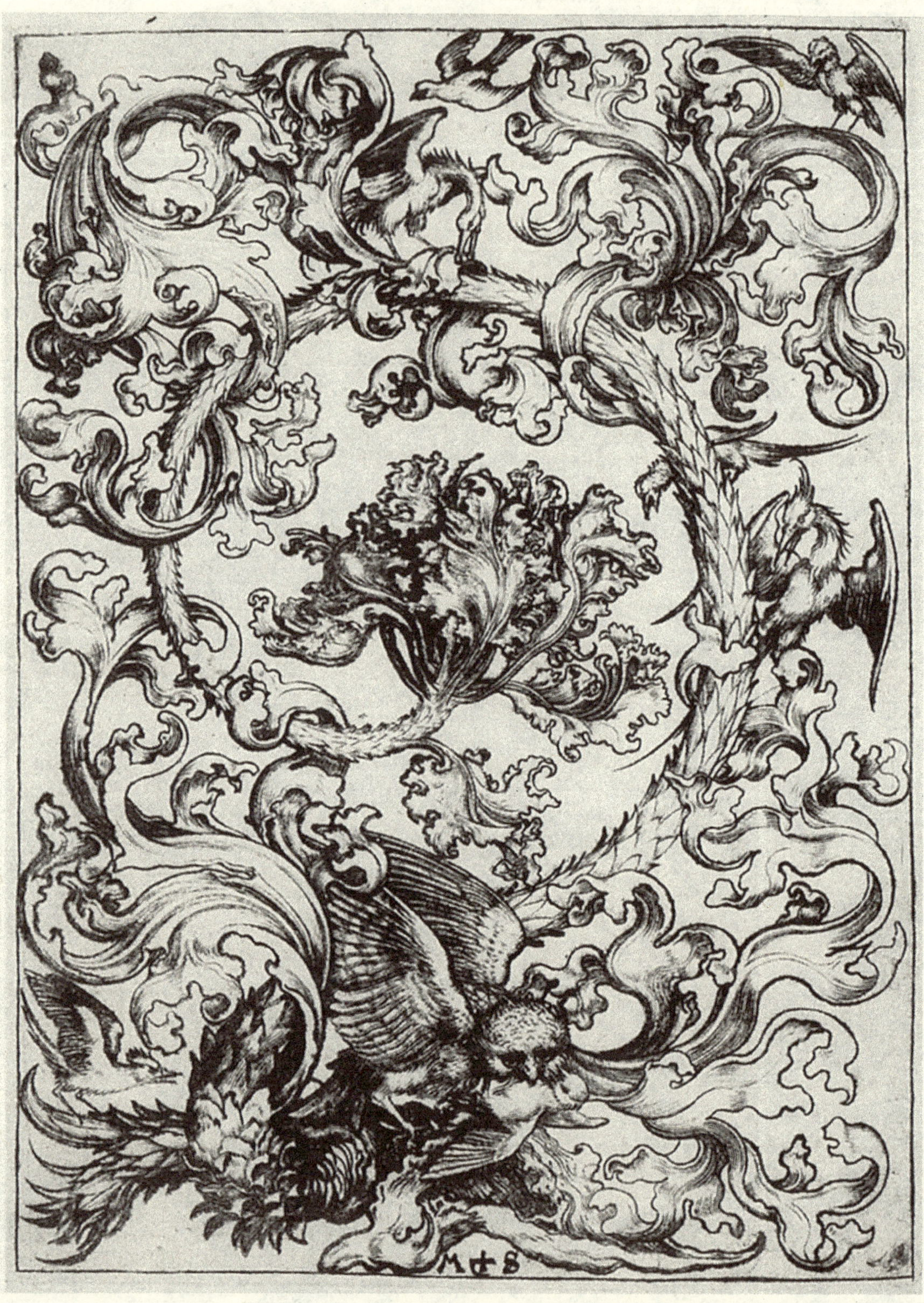

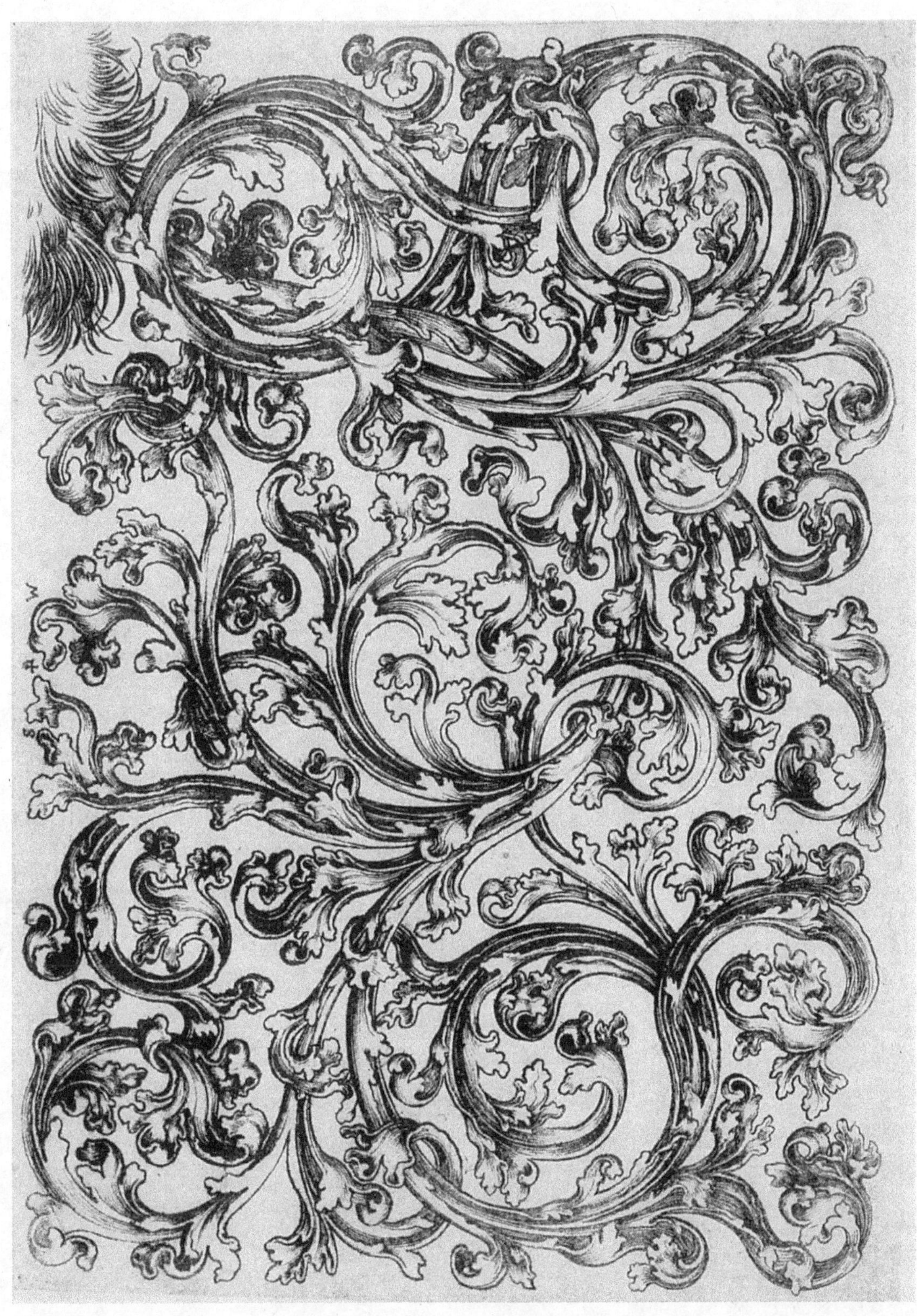

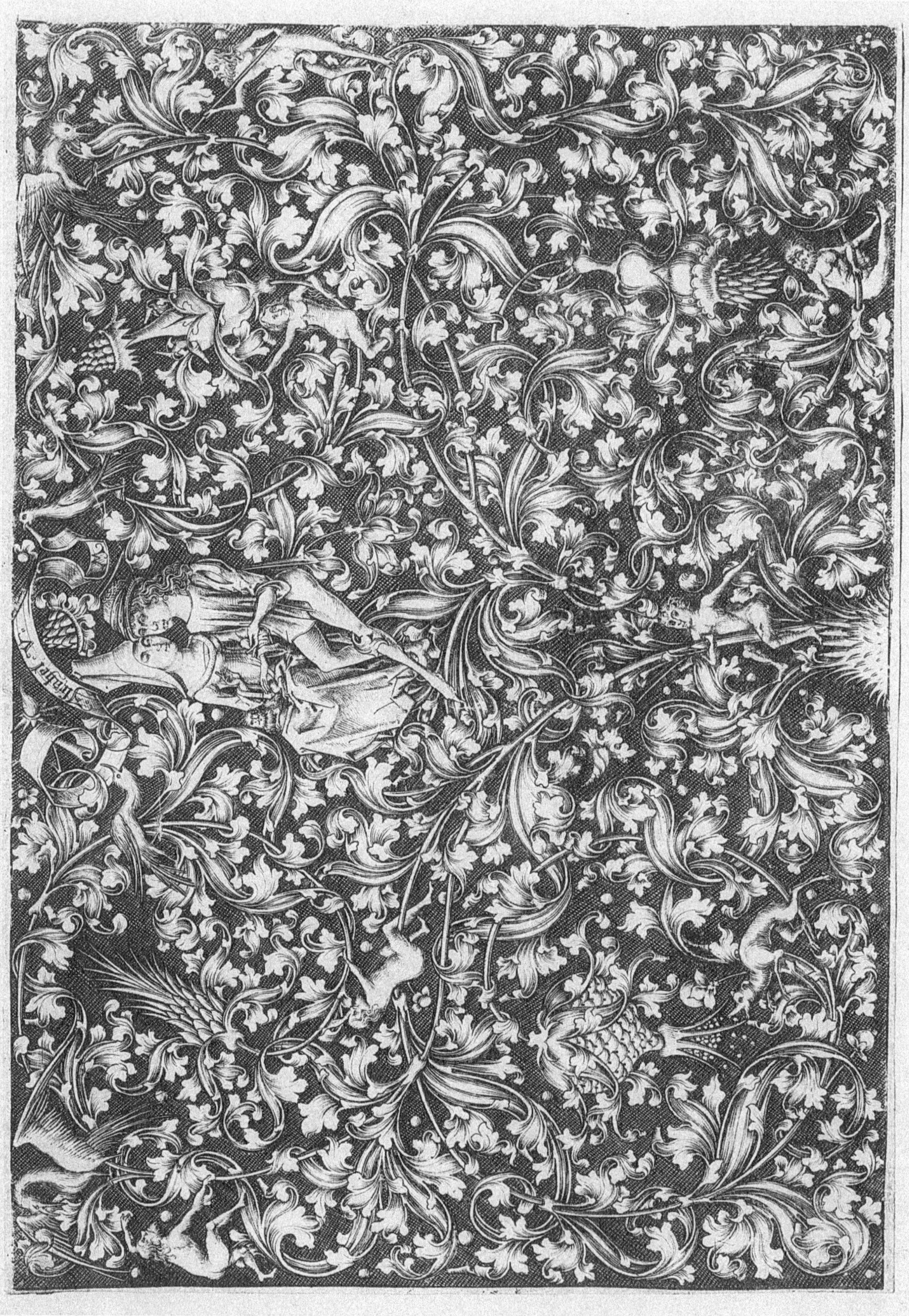

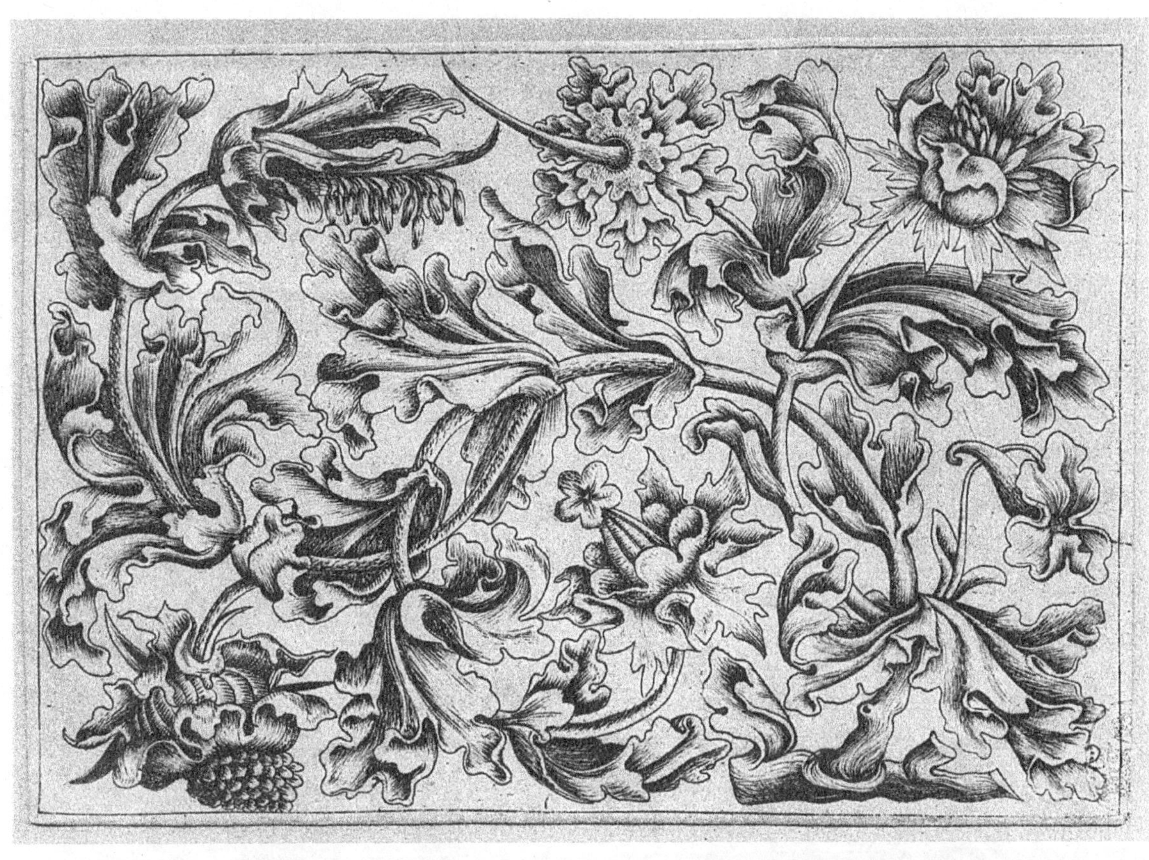

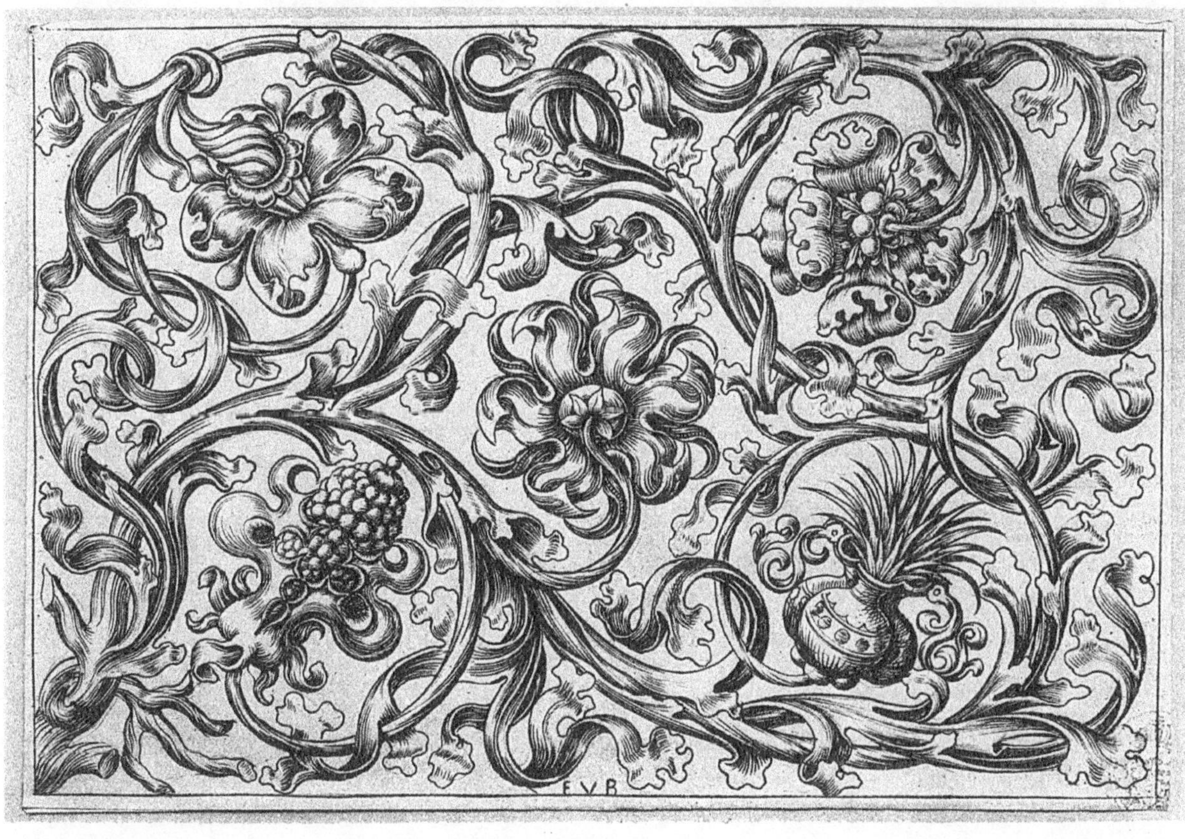
FVB

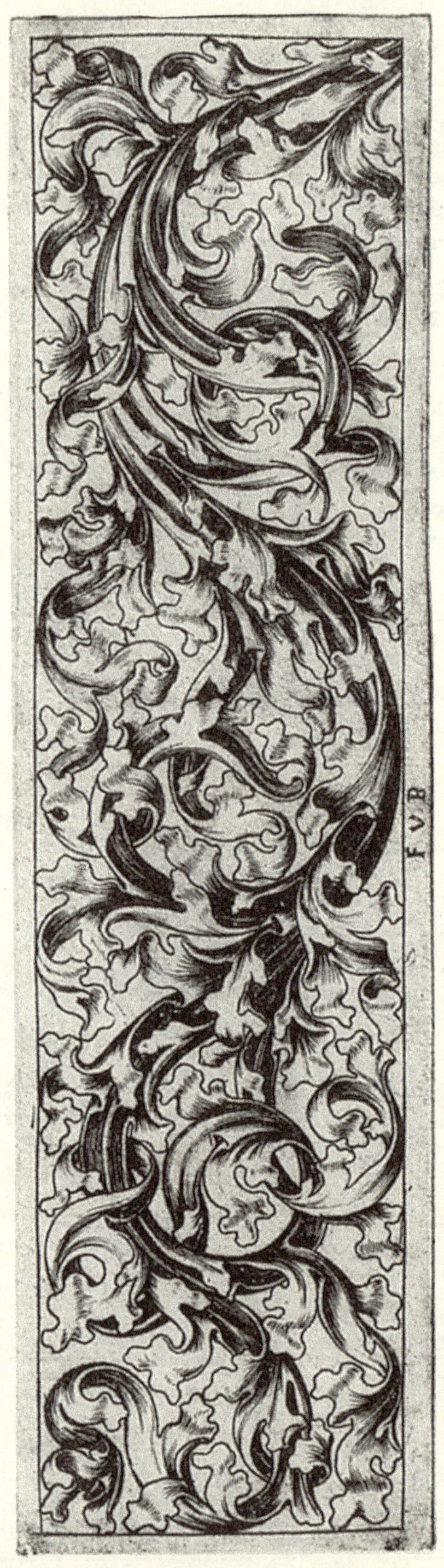
FVB

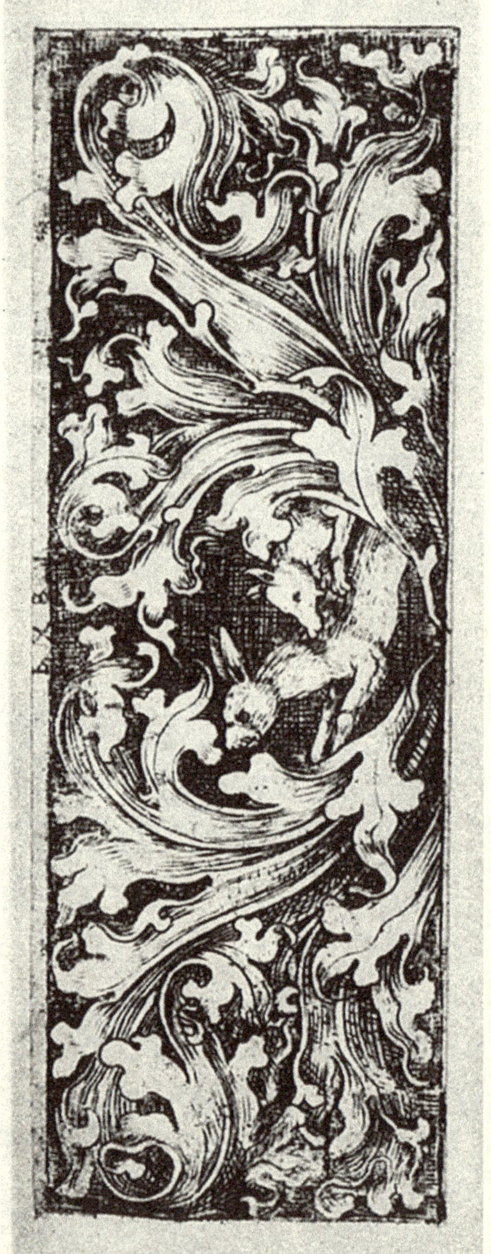

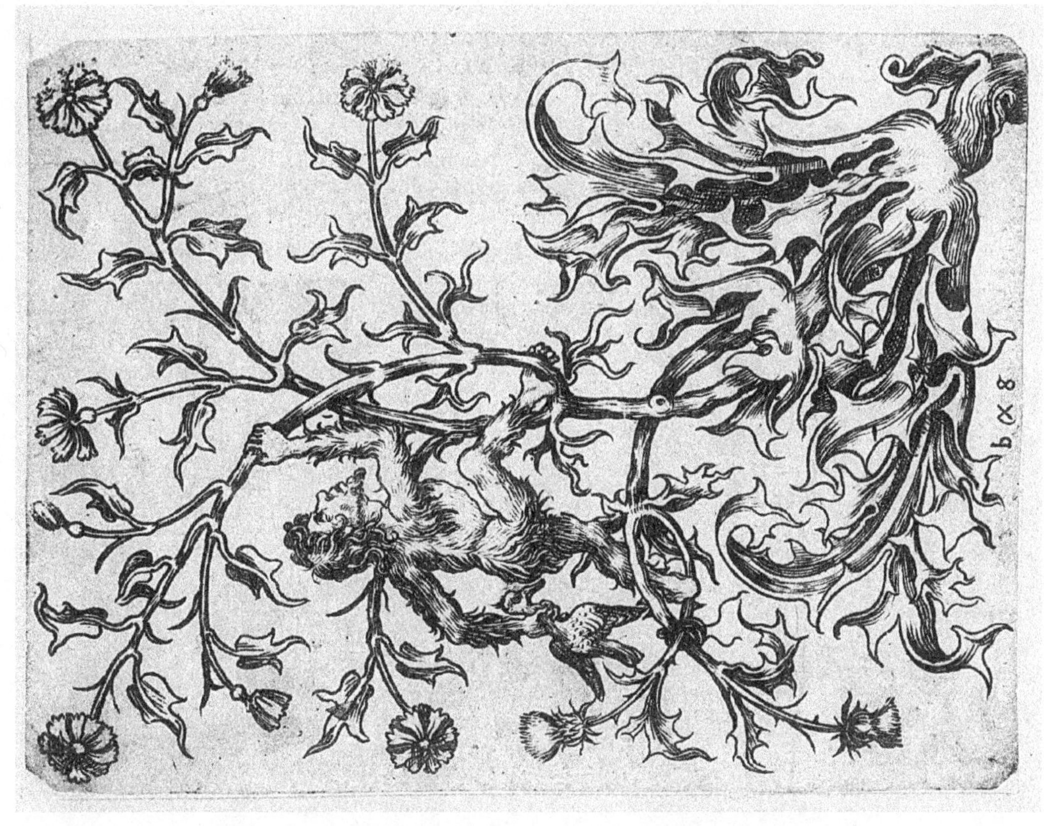

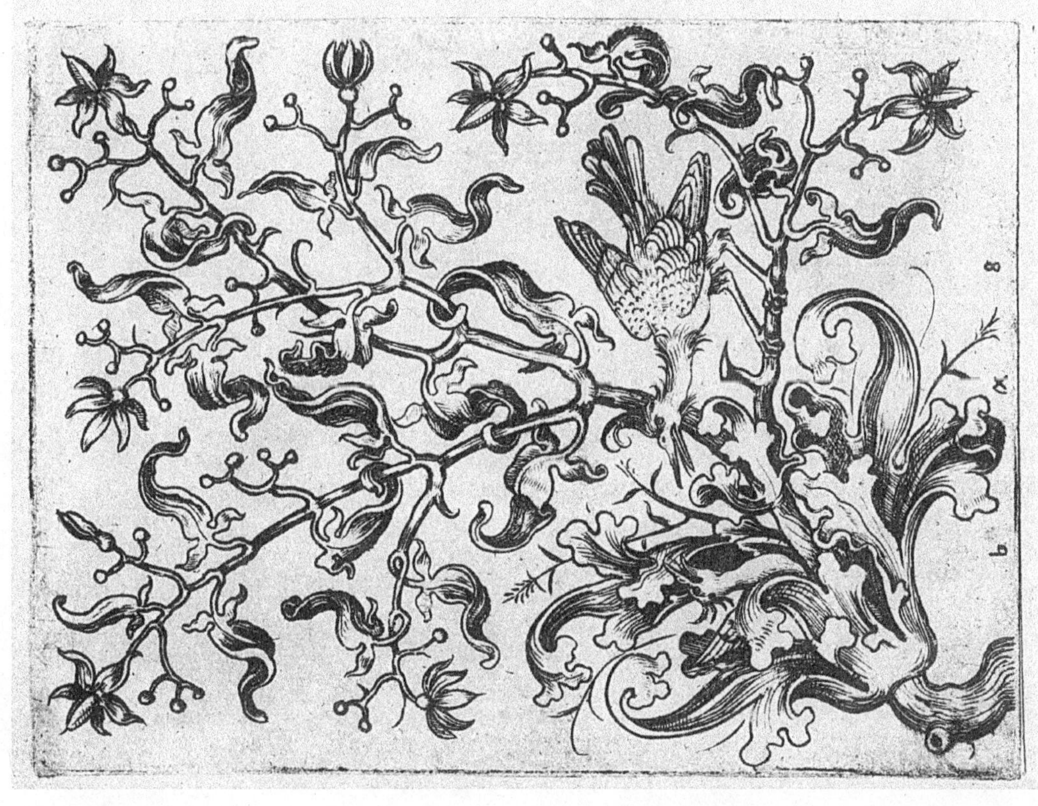

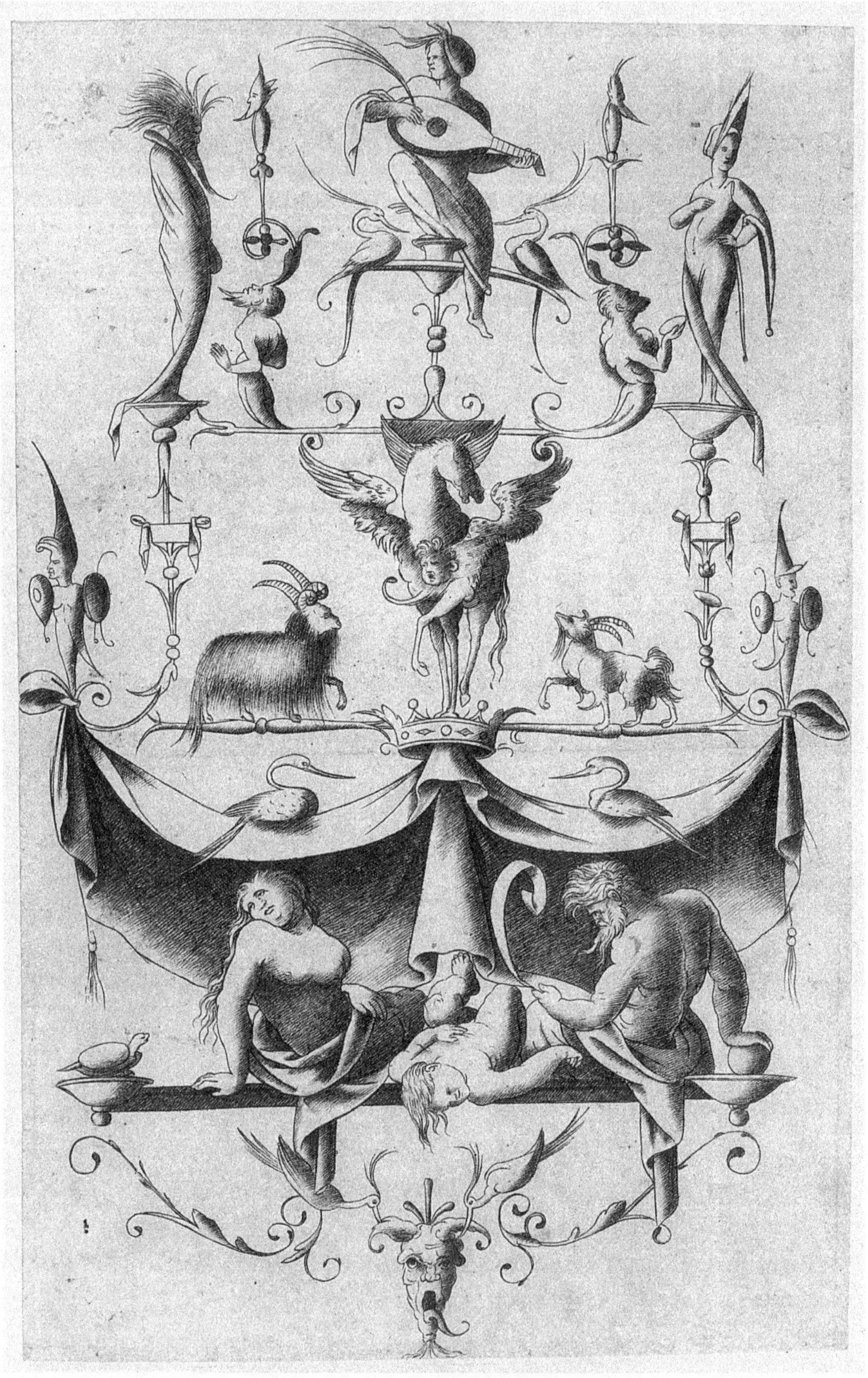

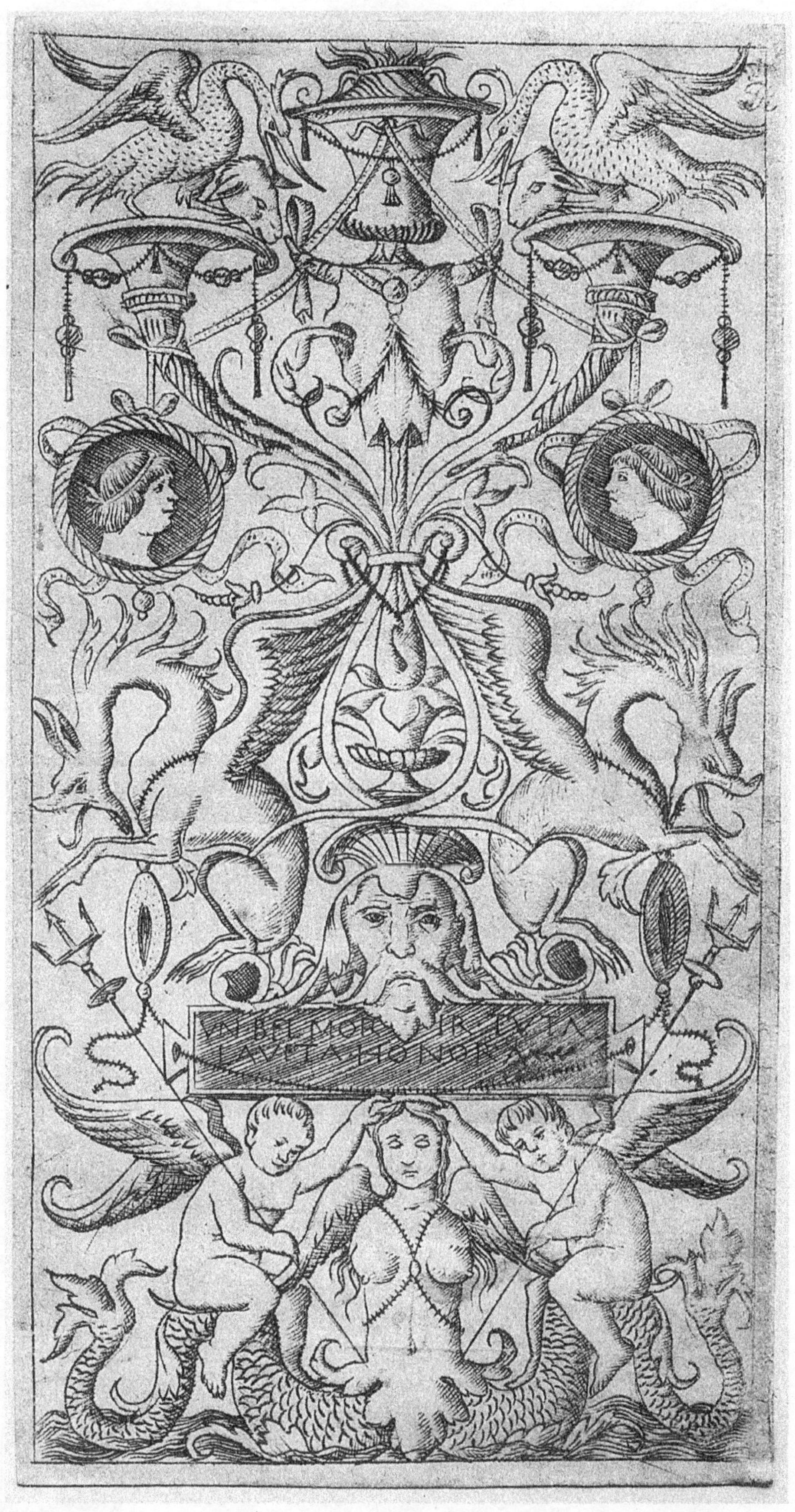
VN BEL MOR IR TVTA
LAVITA HONORA

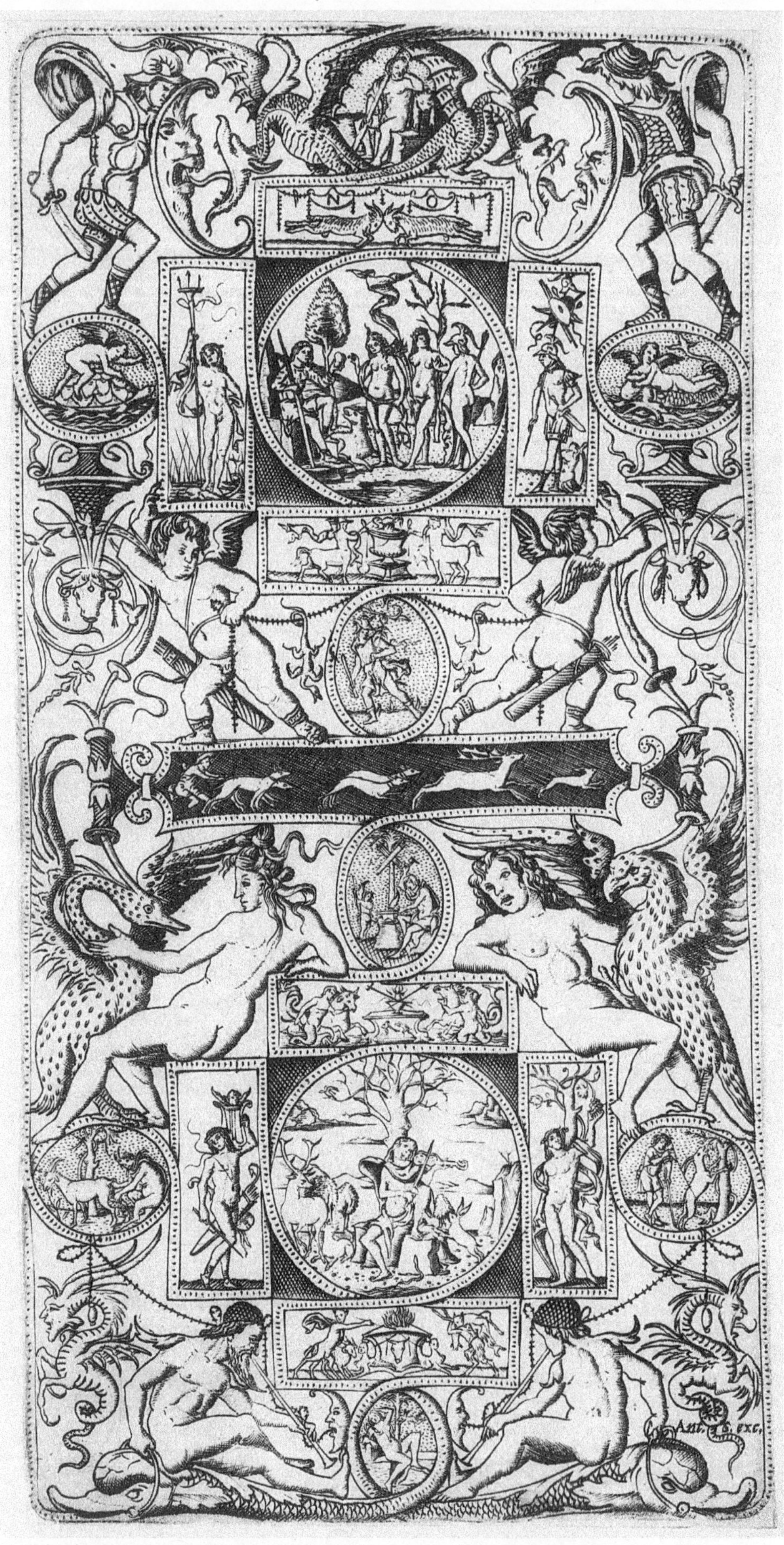

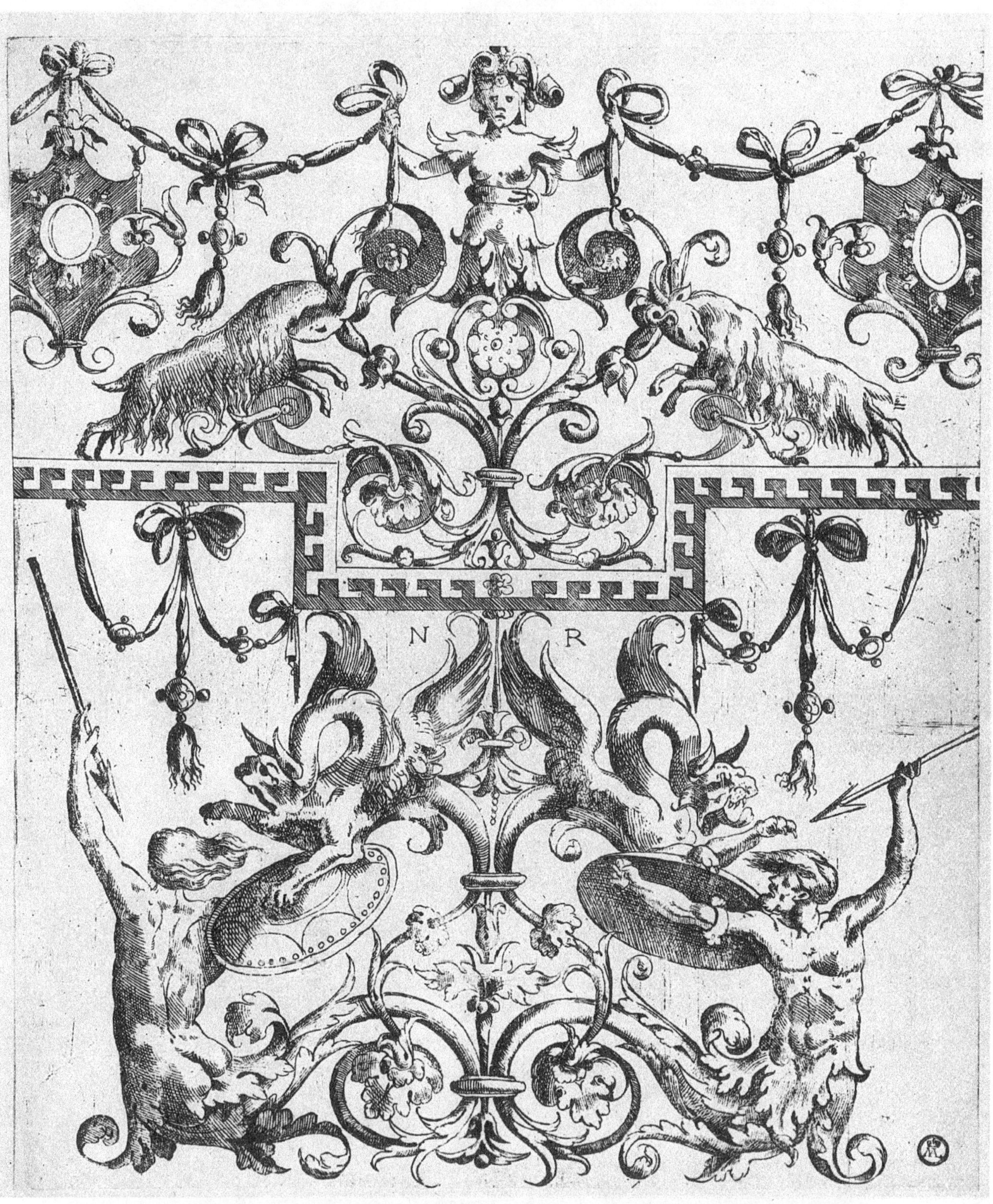
N R

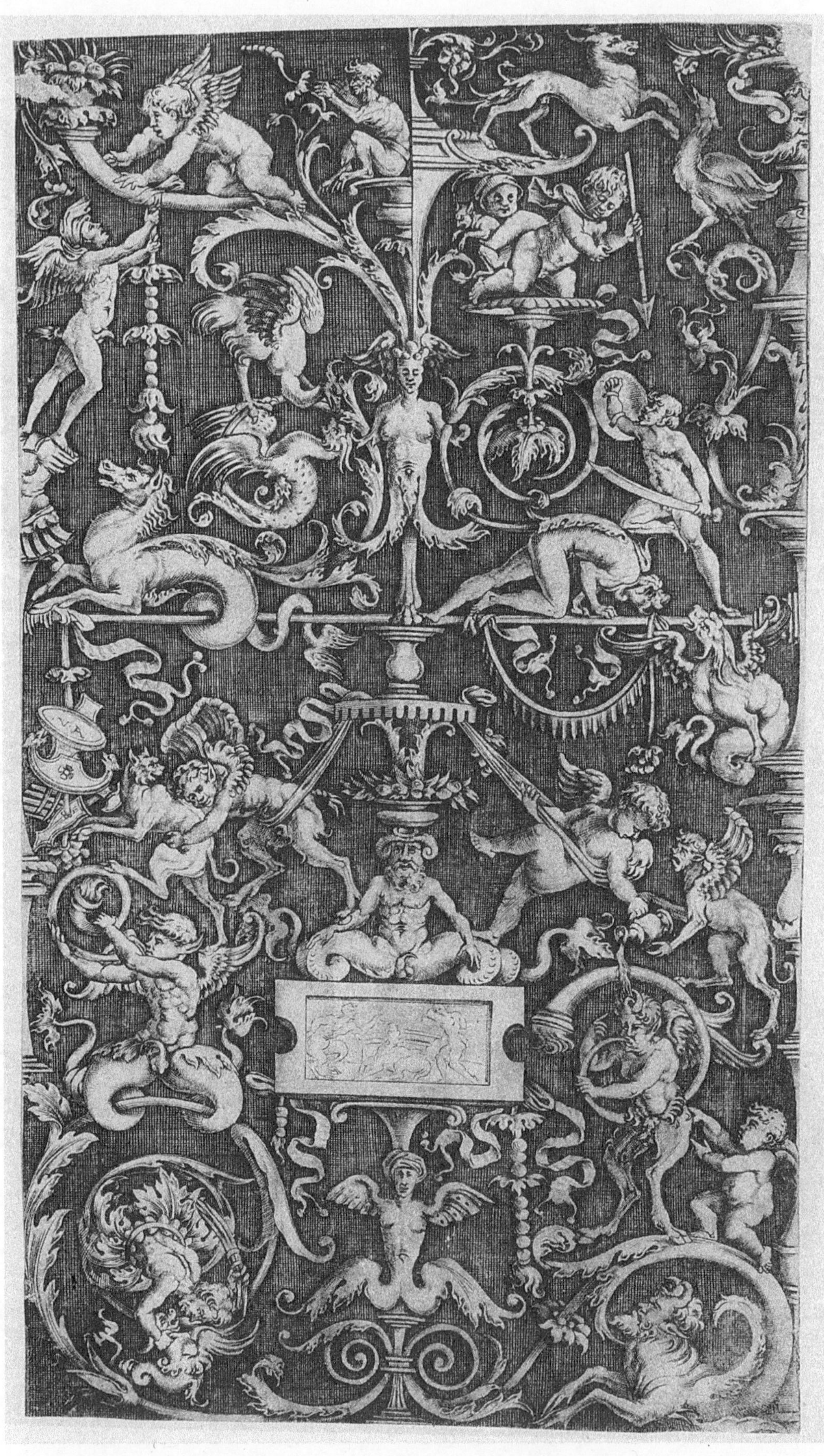

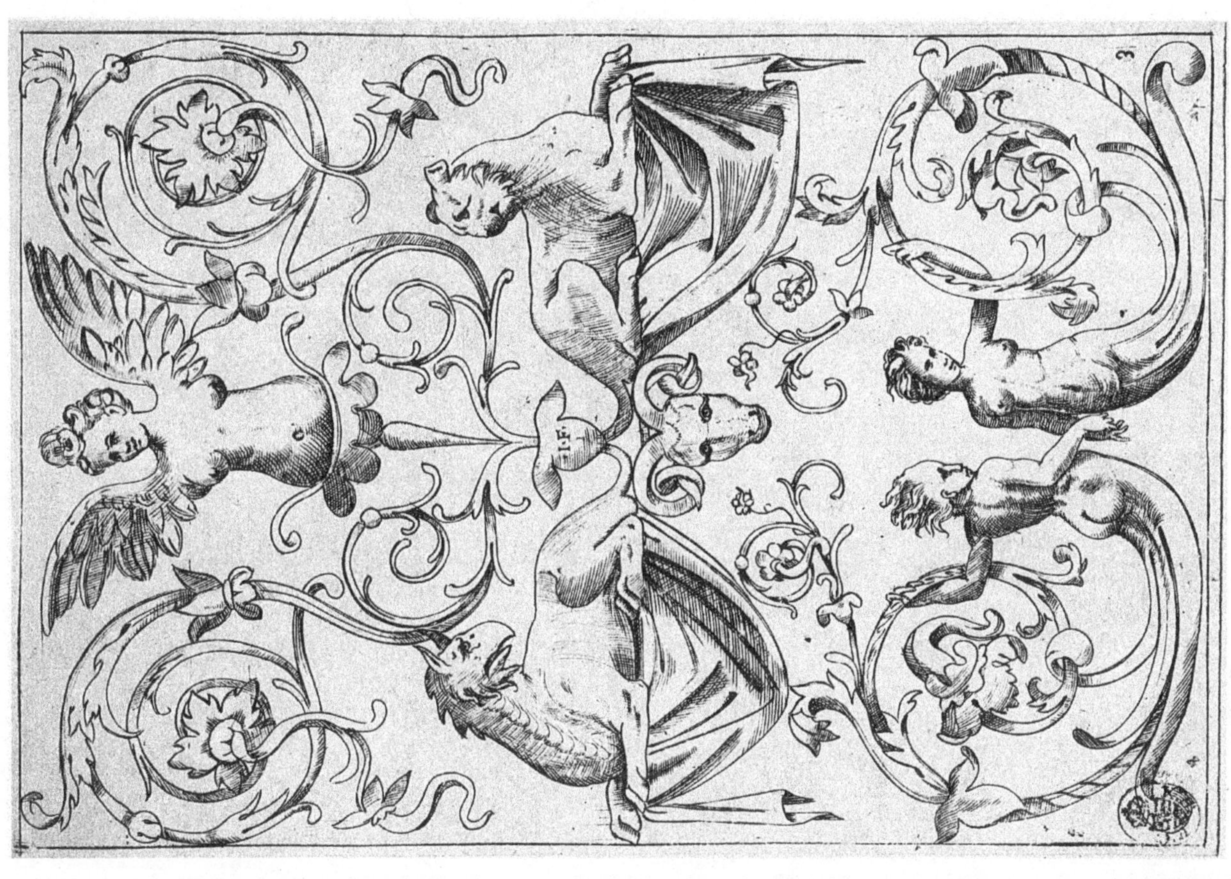

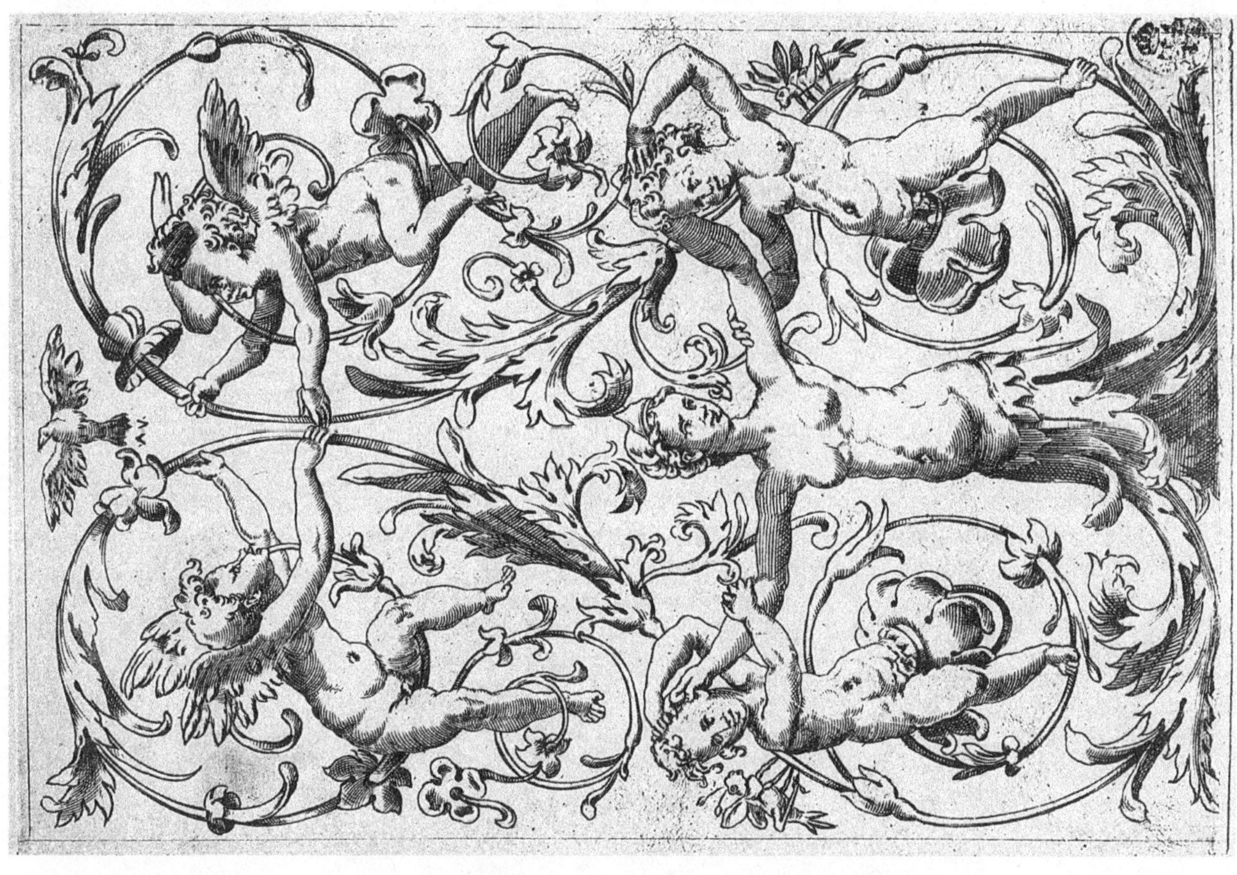

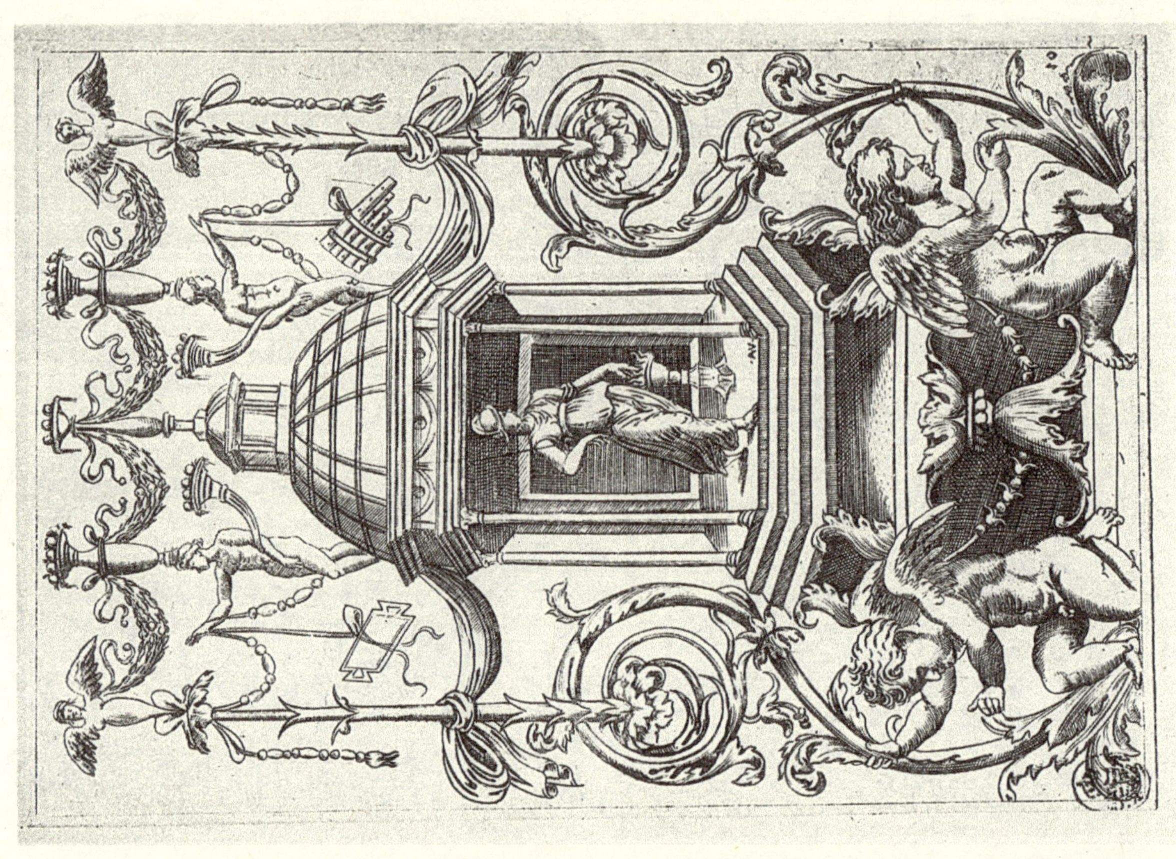

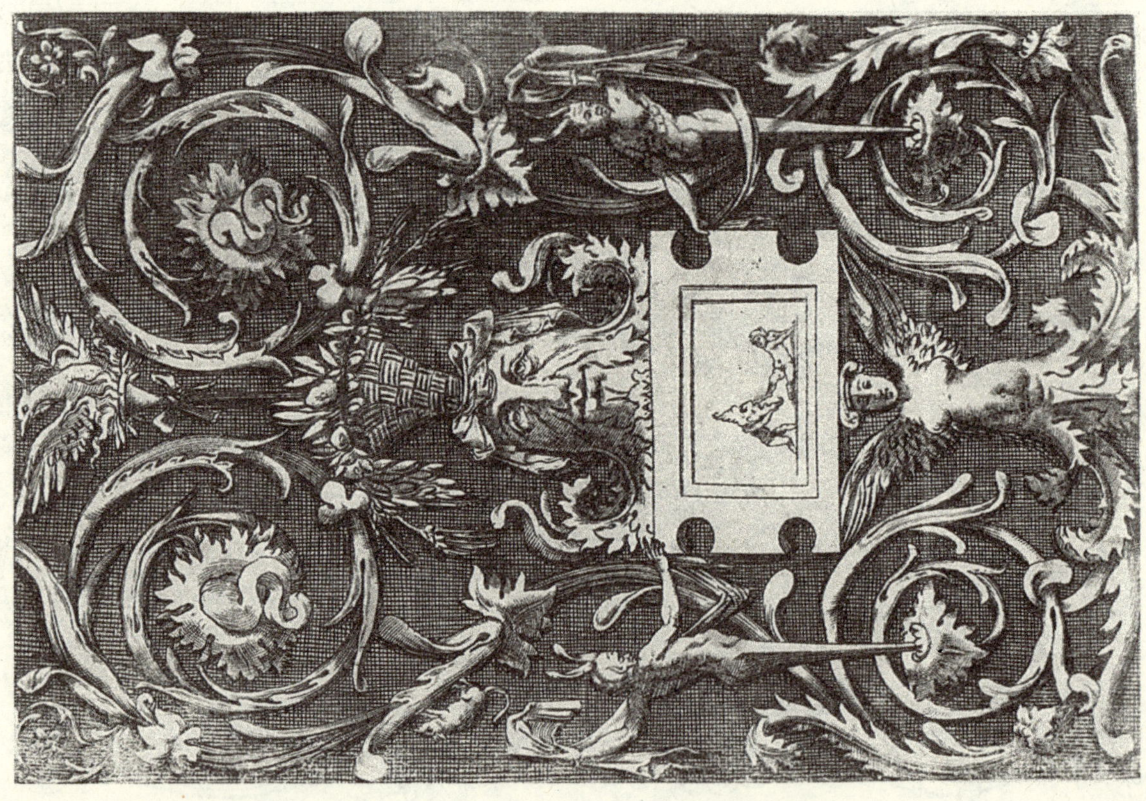

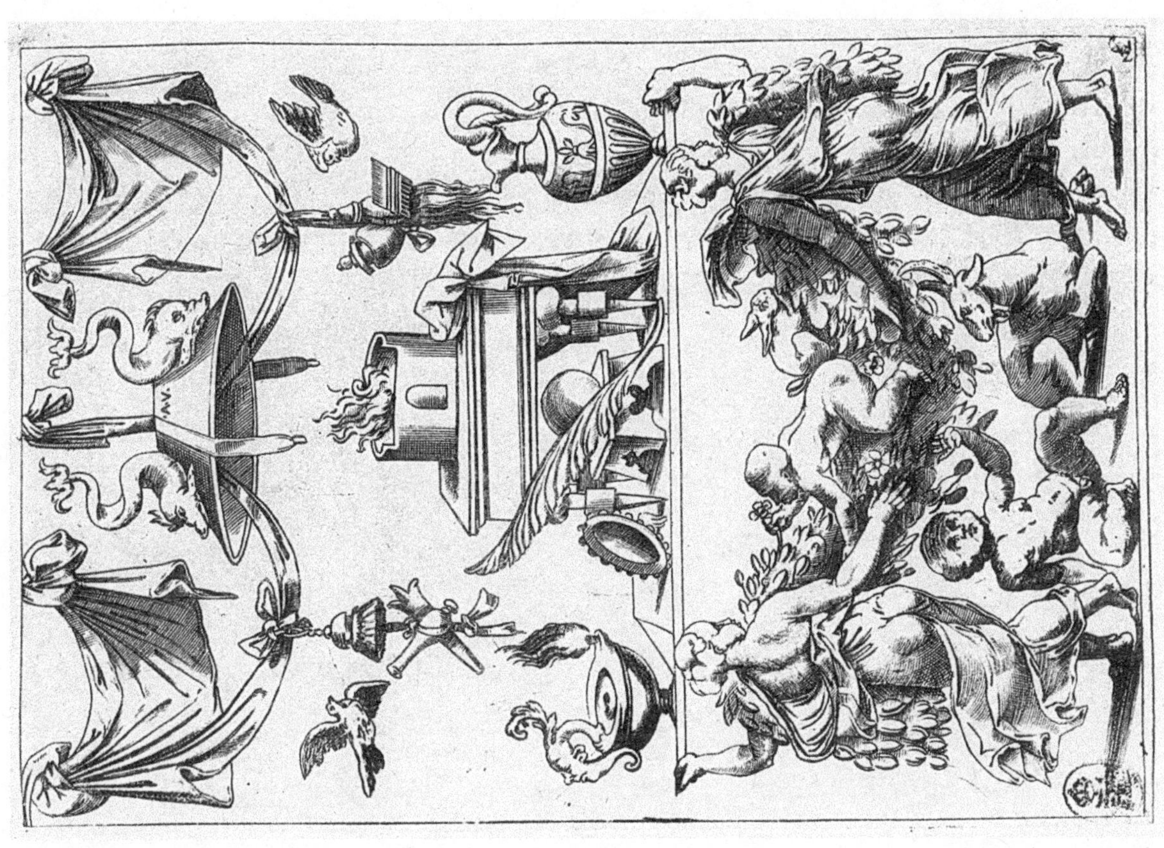

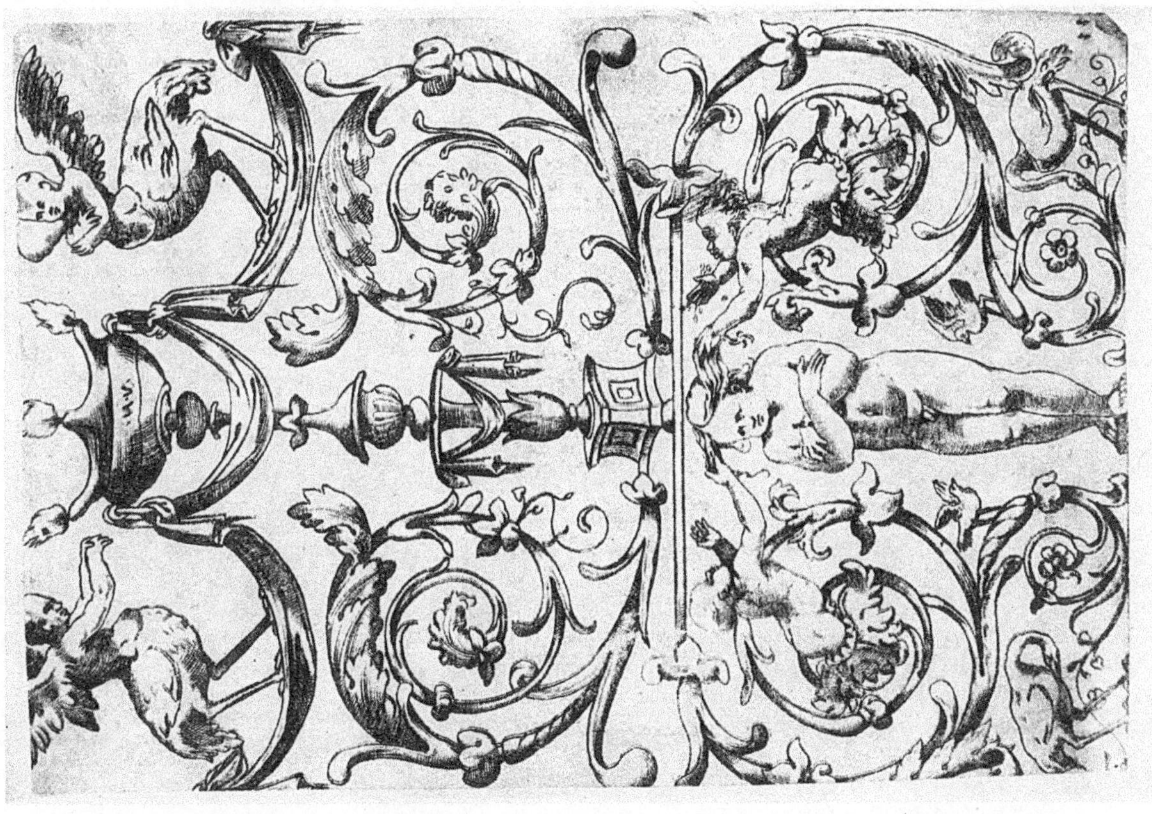

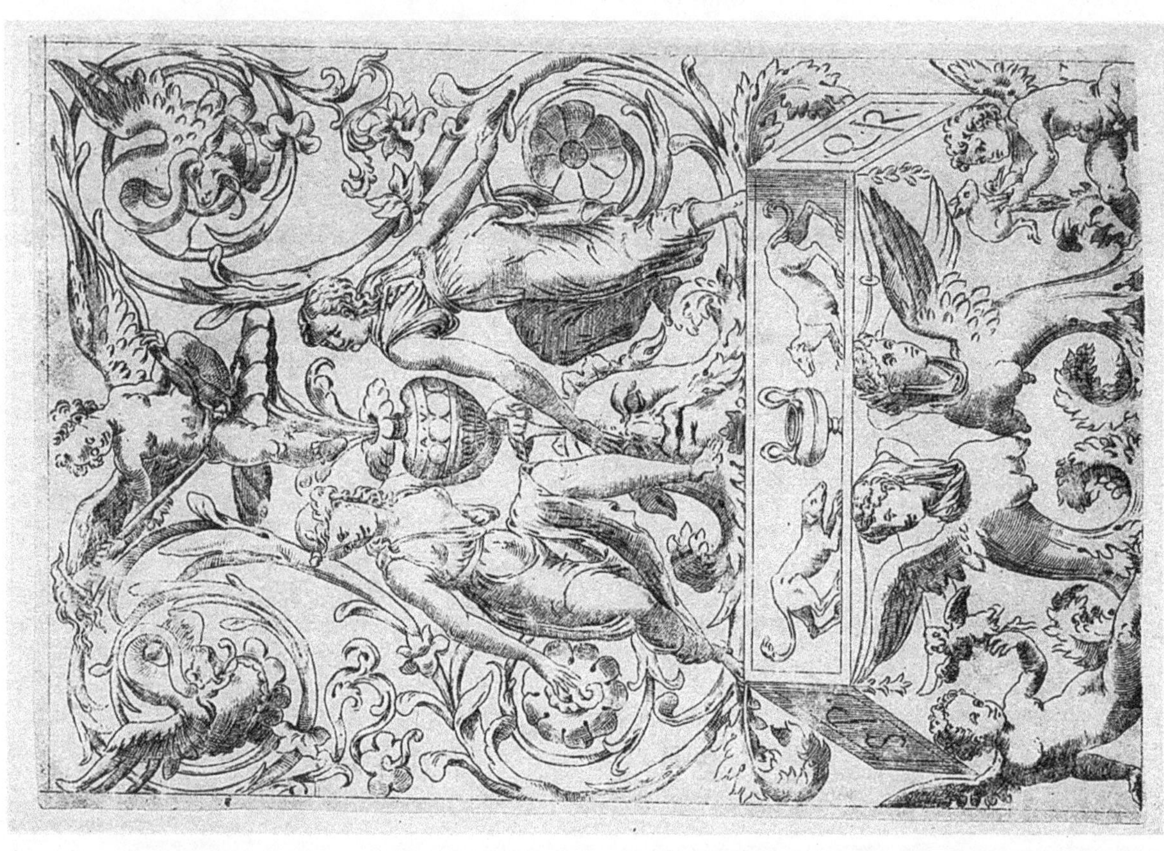

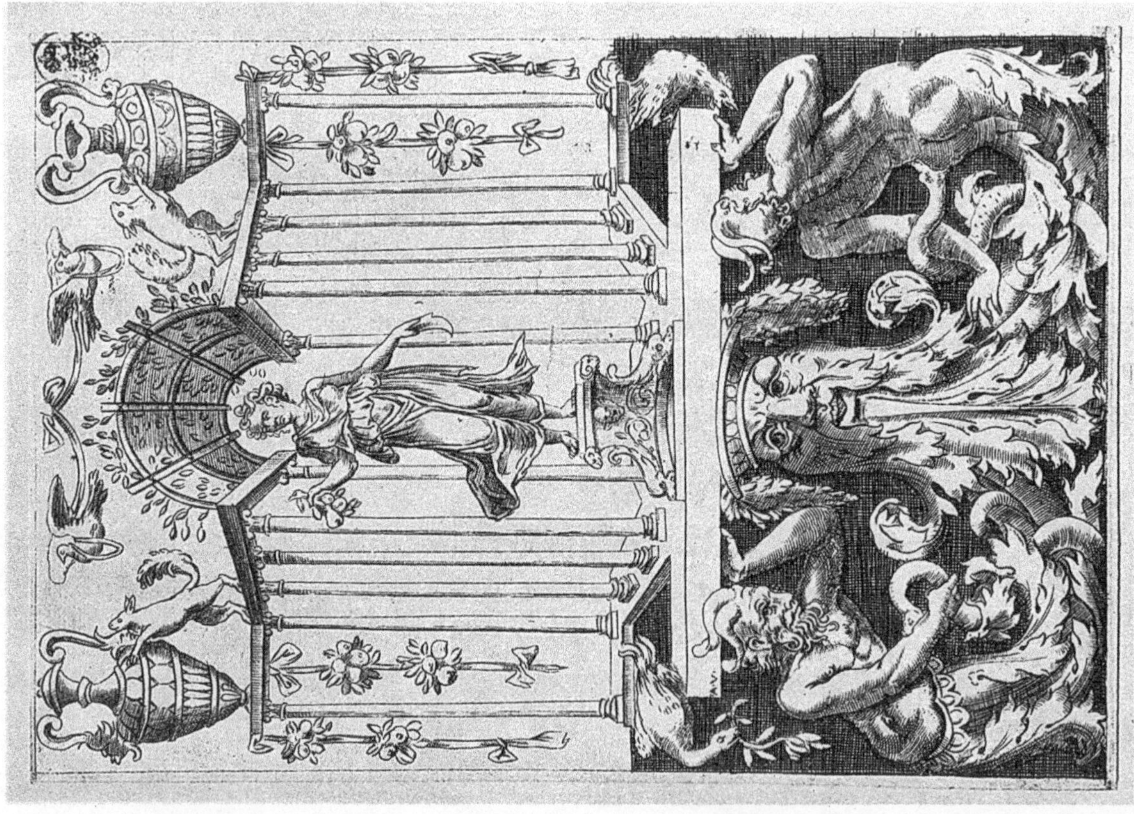

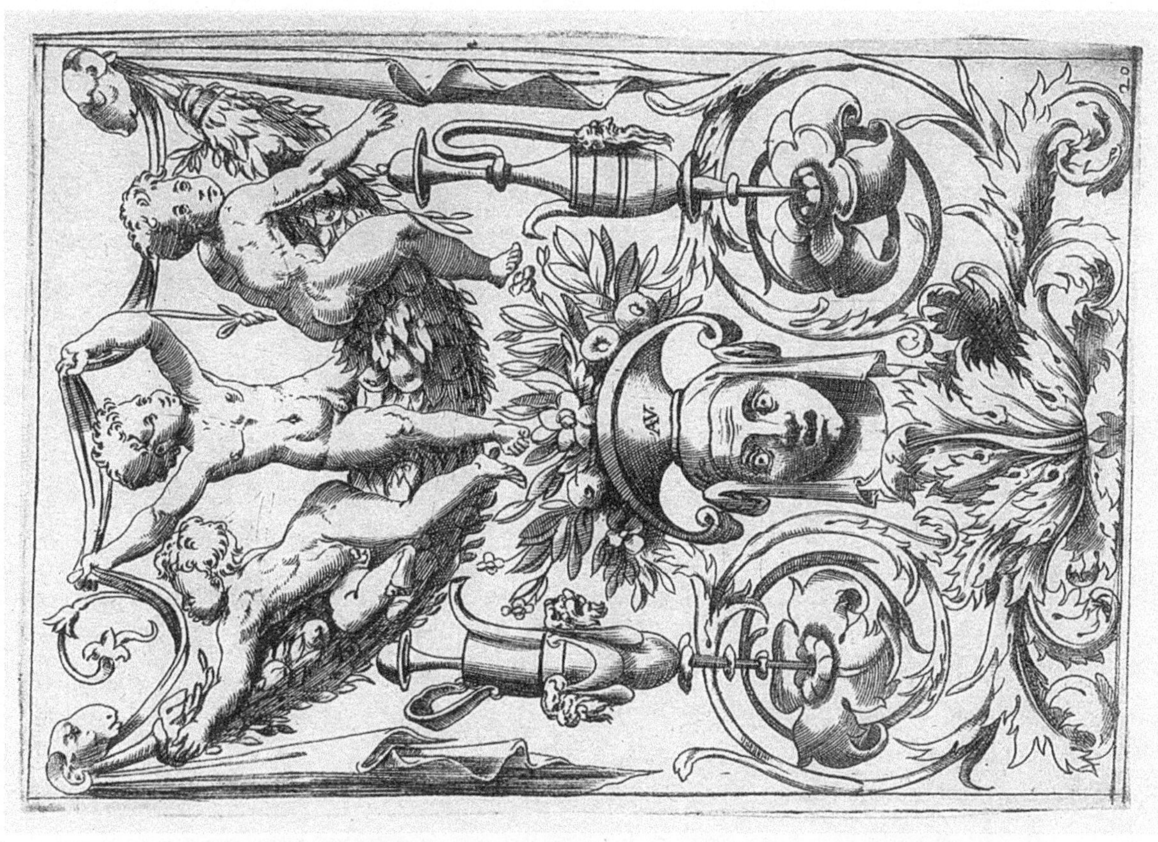

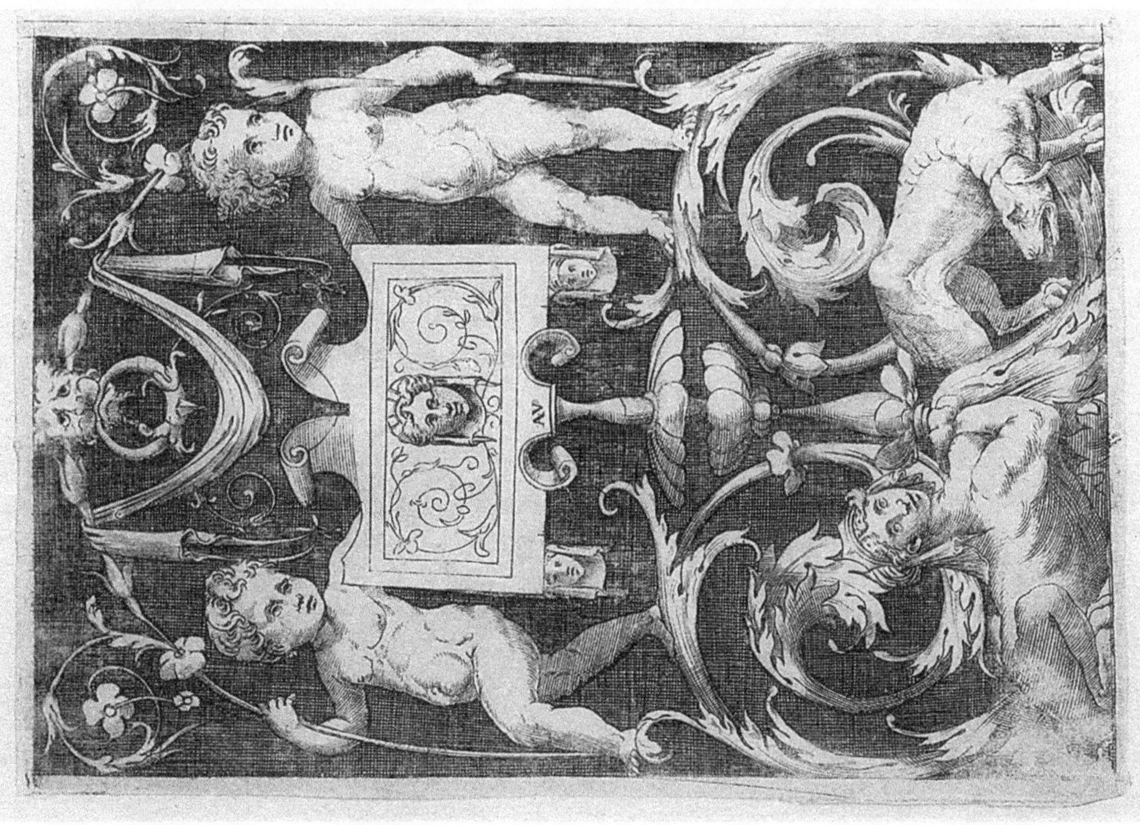

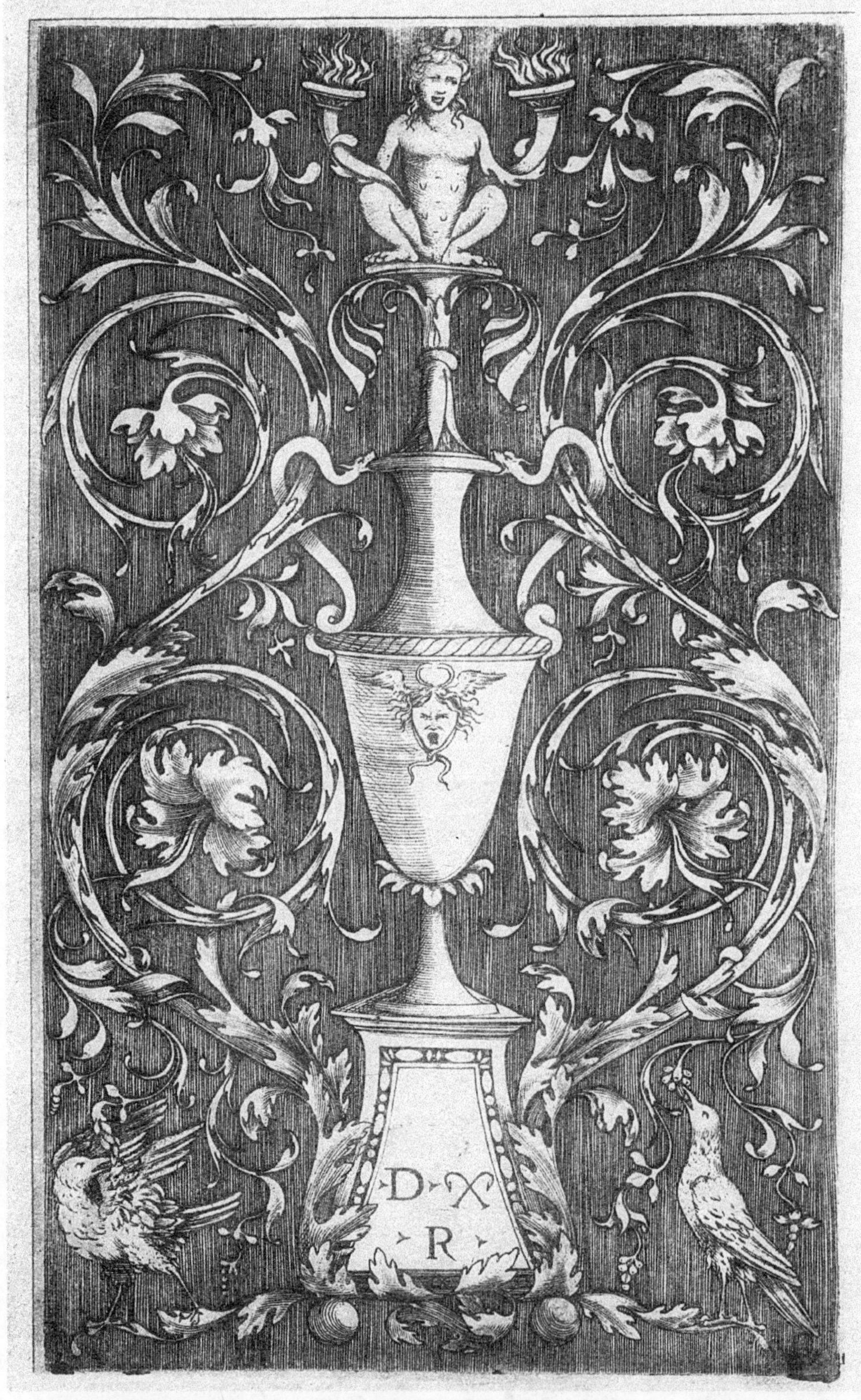
D X
R

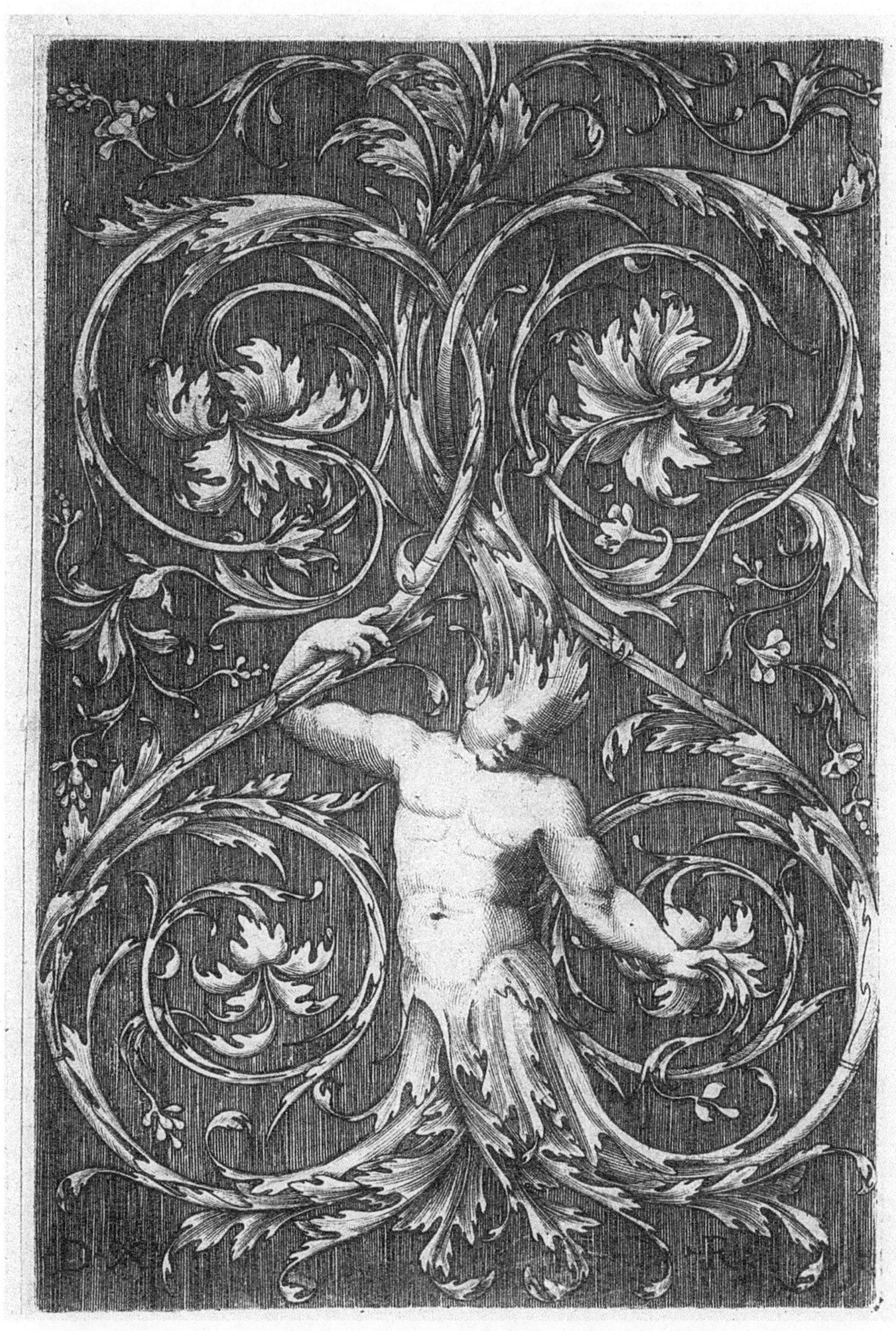

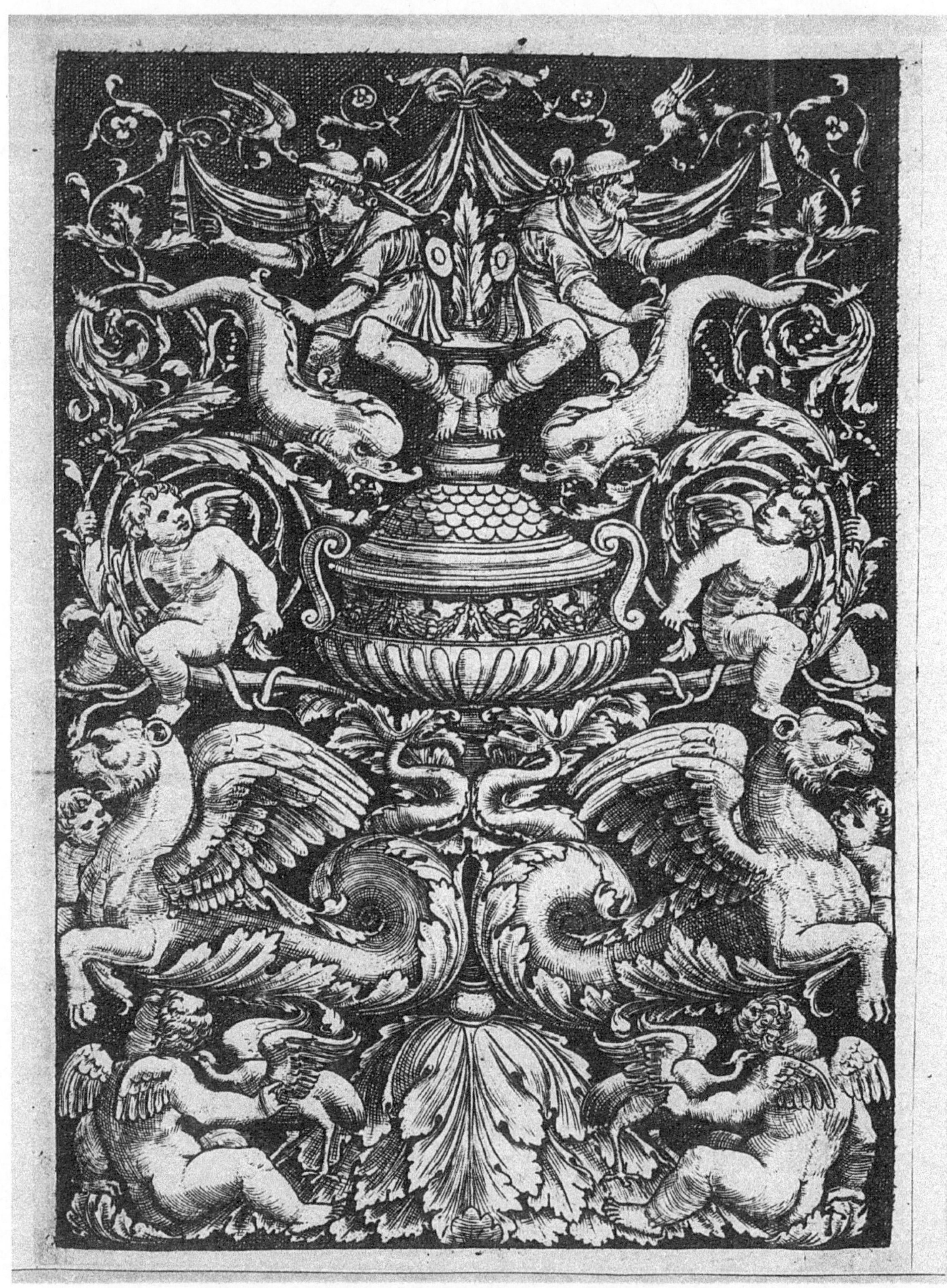

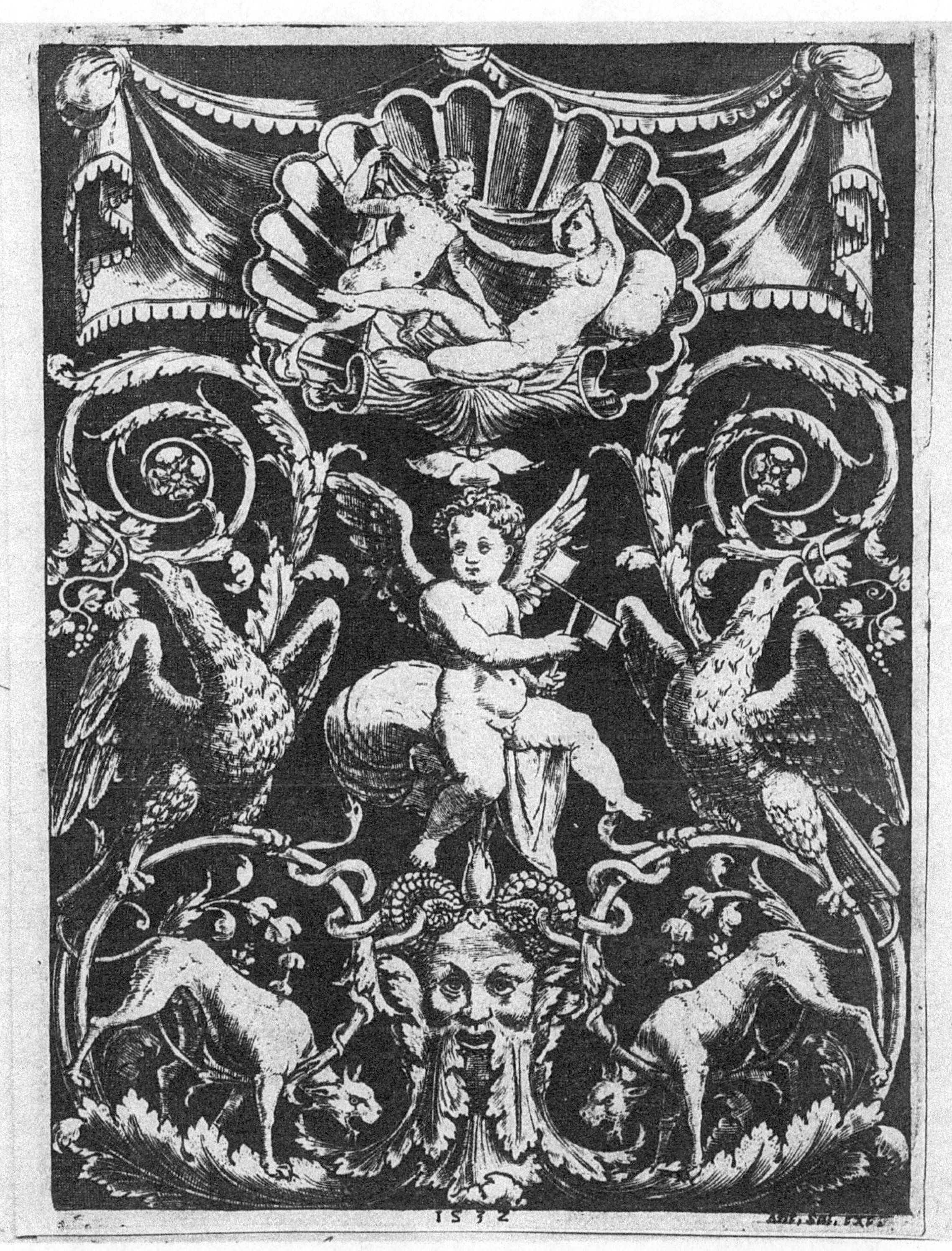
1532

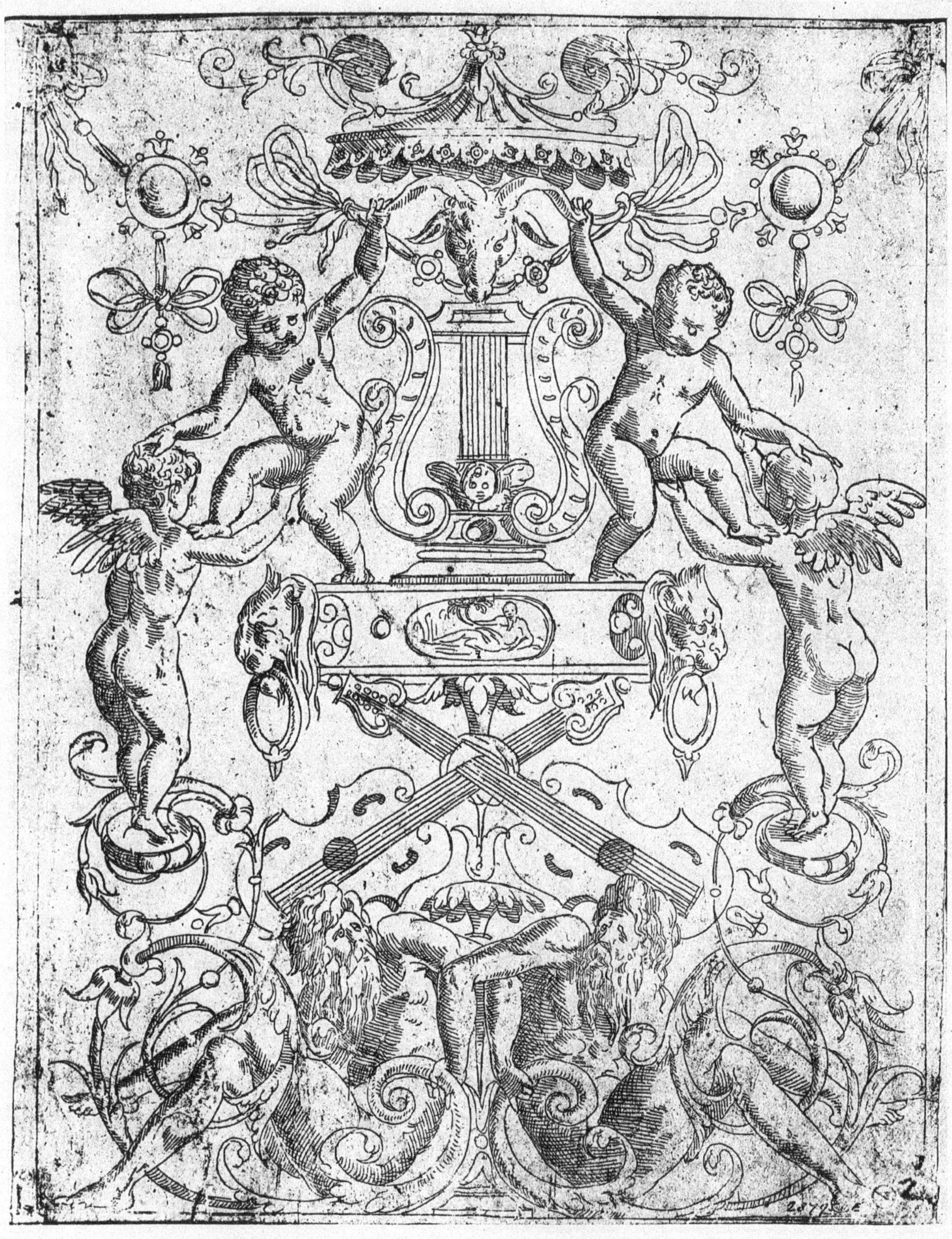

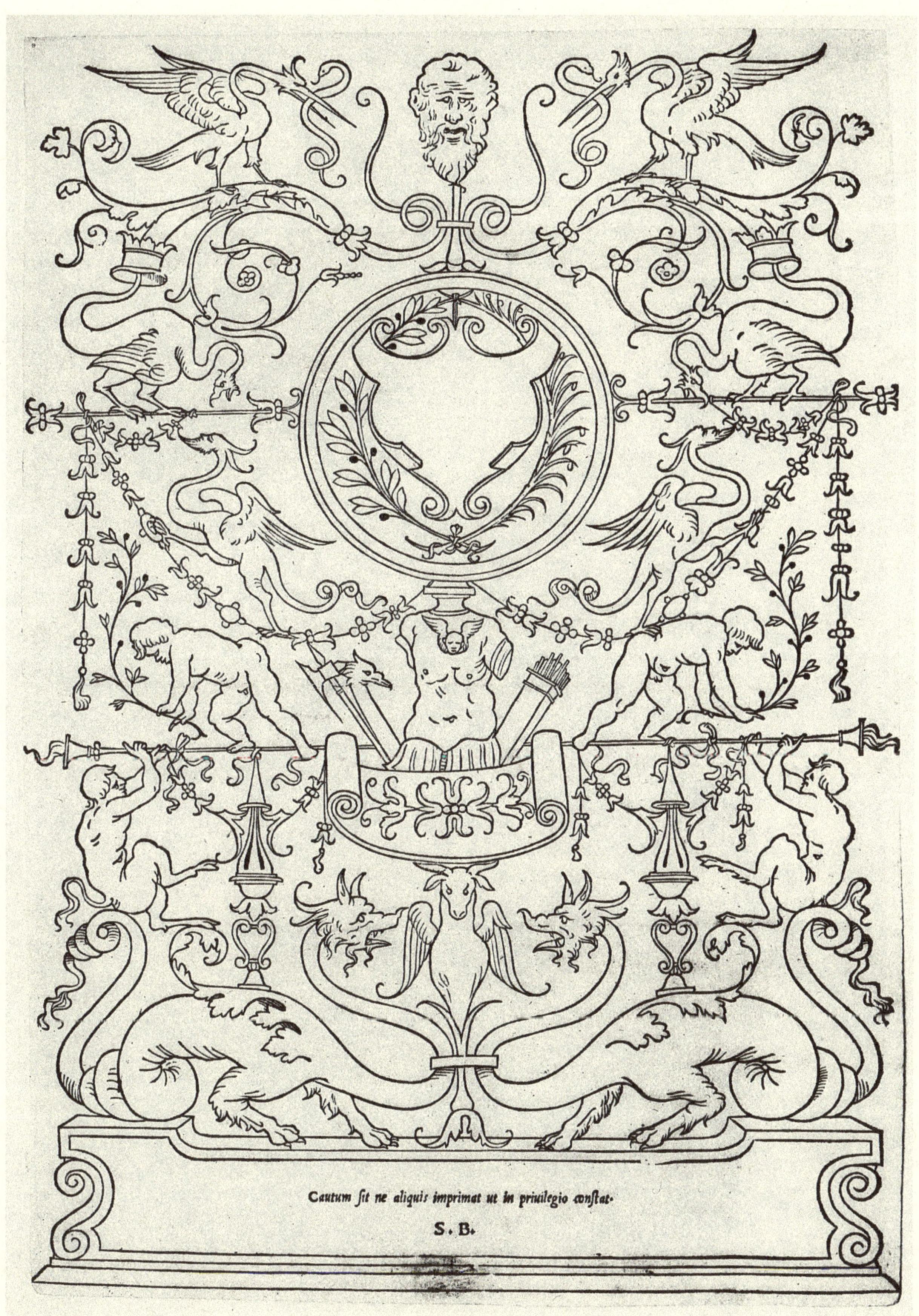
Cautum sit ne aliquis imprimat ut in priuilegio constat.
S. B.

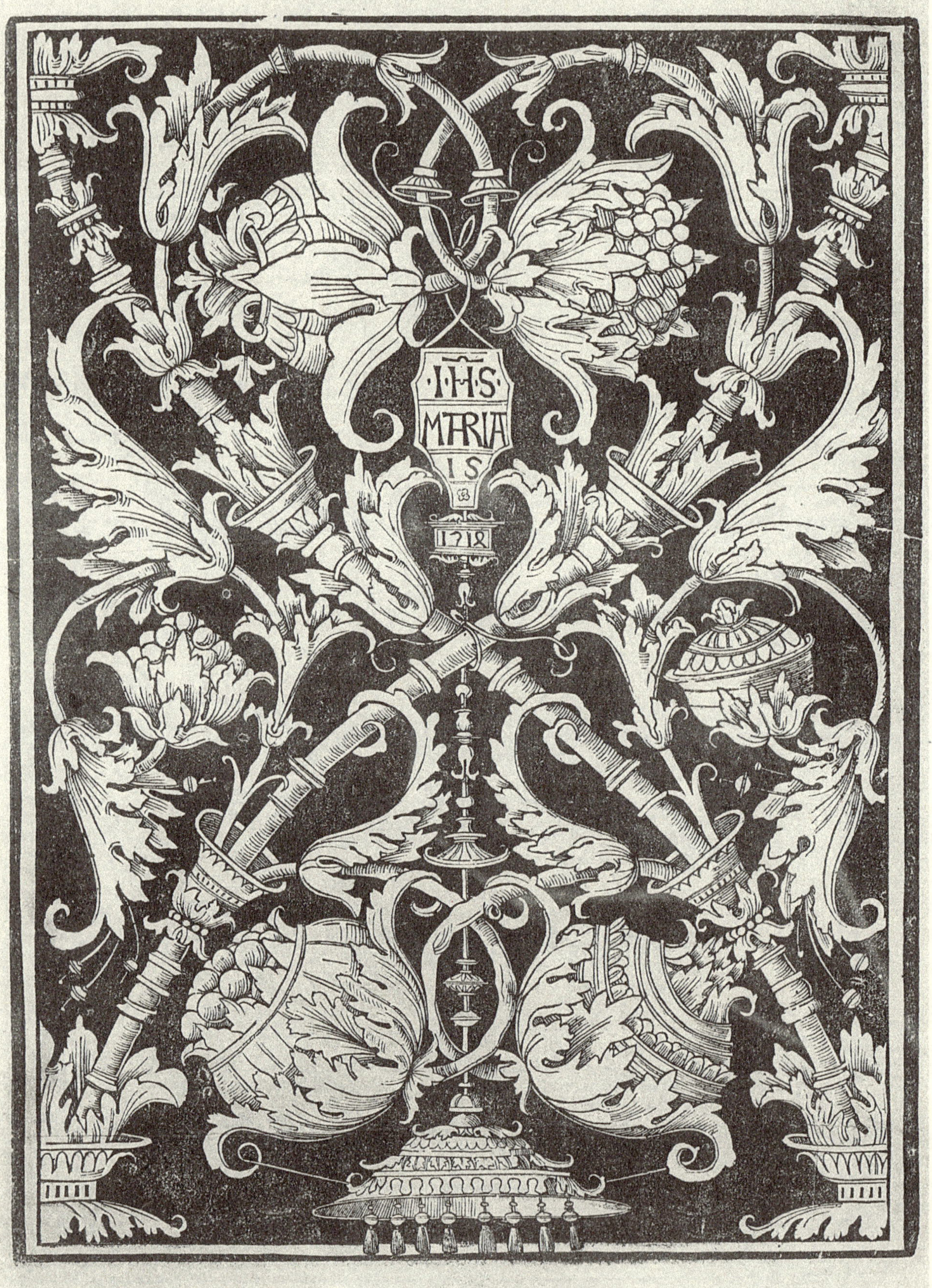
·I·H·S·
MARIA
IS
1718

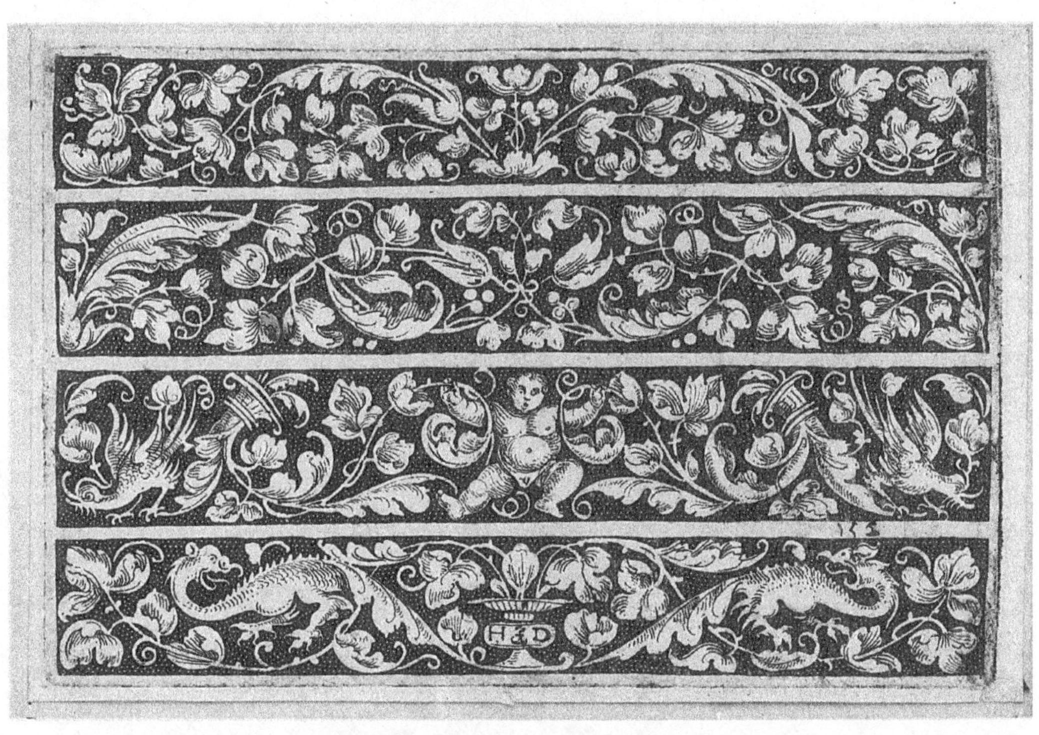

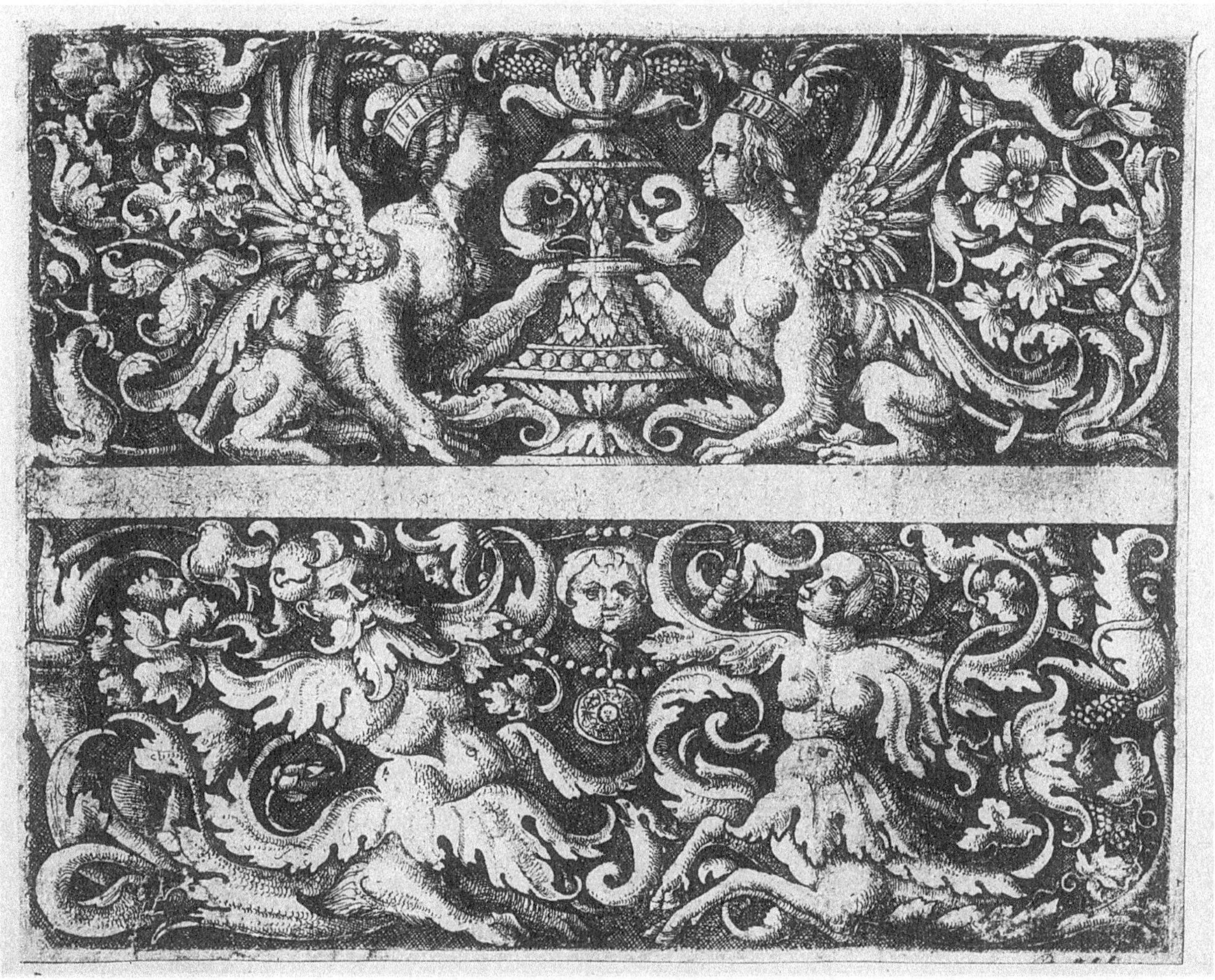

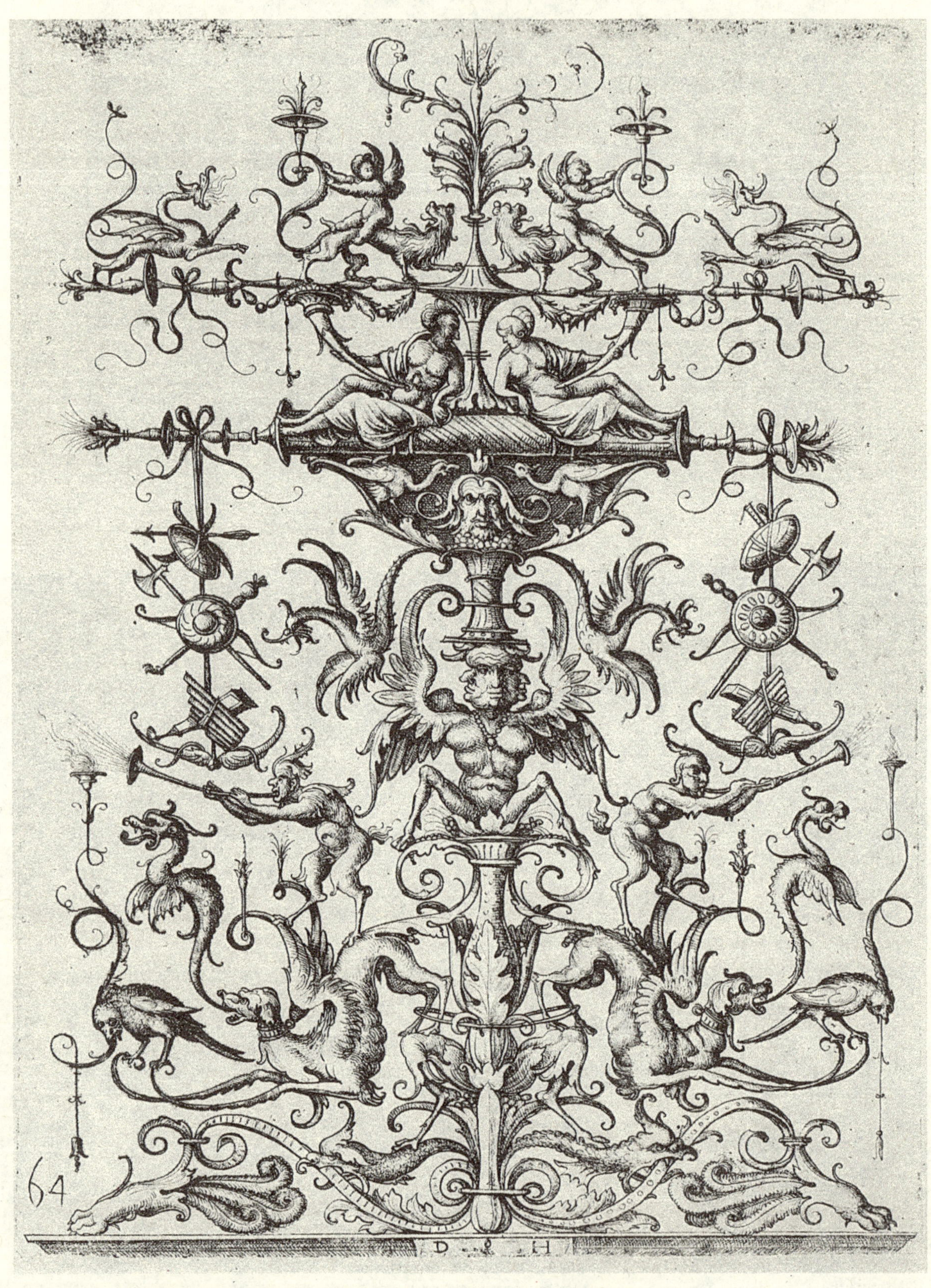
64
D H

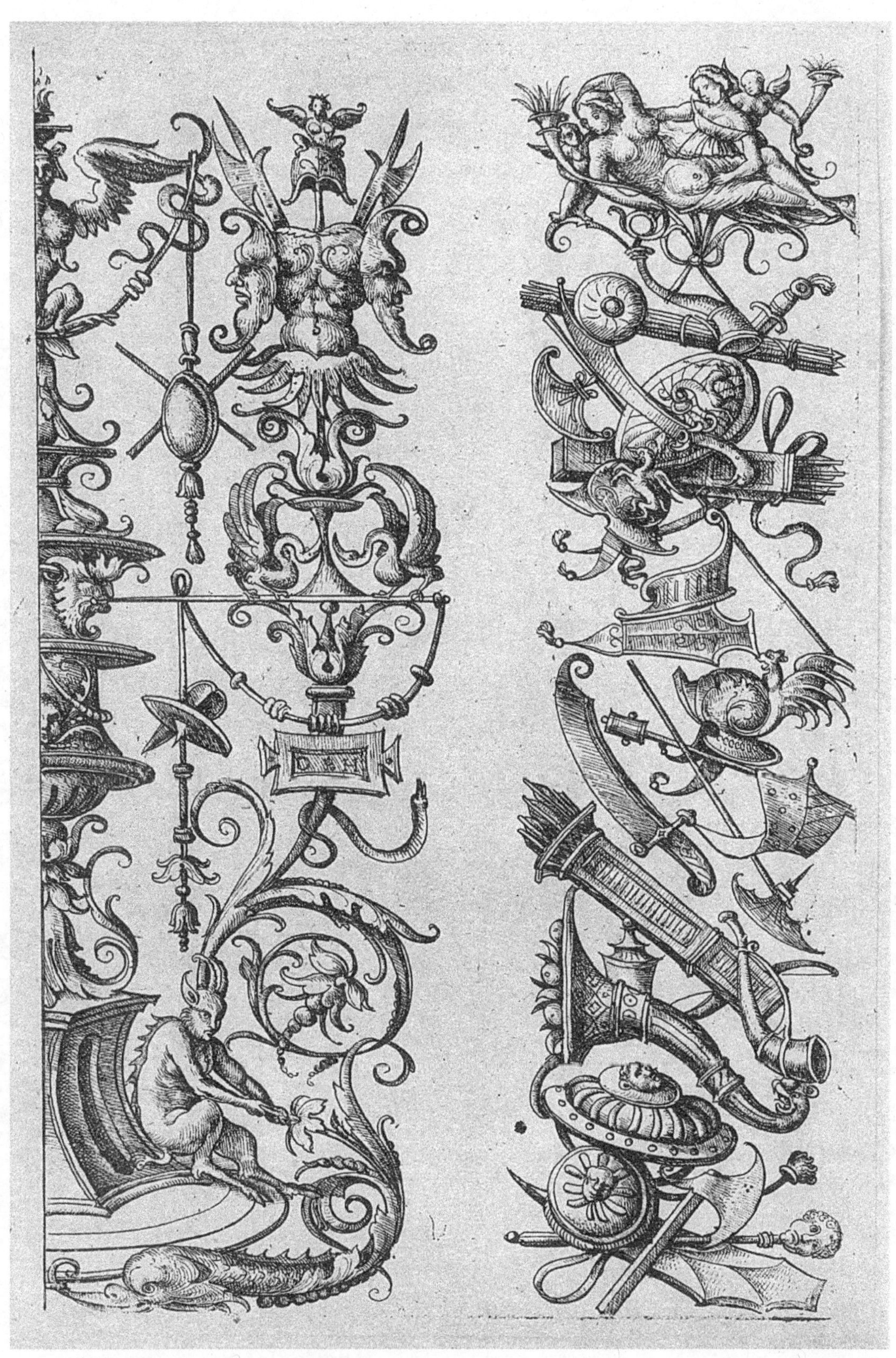

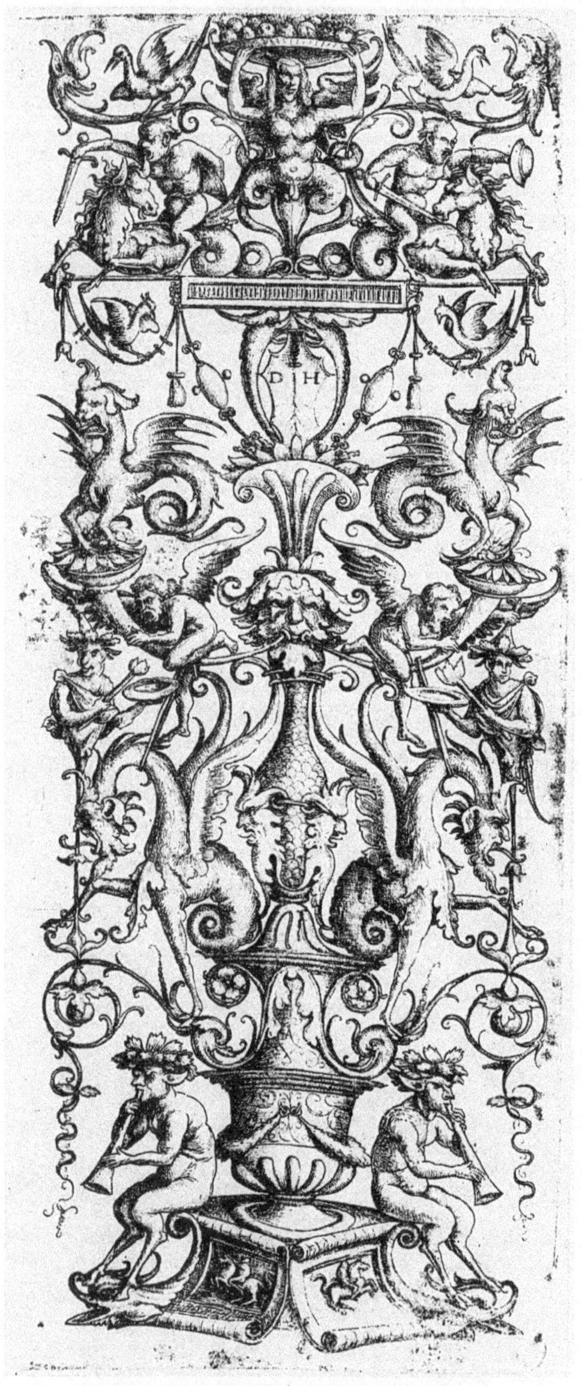

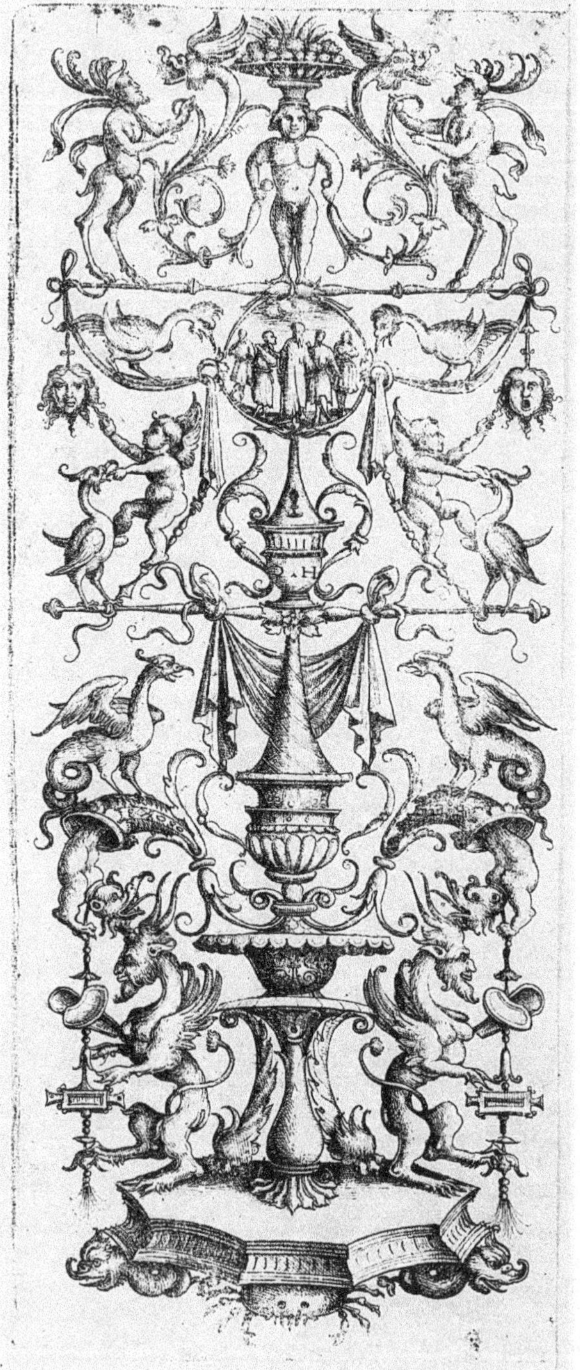

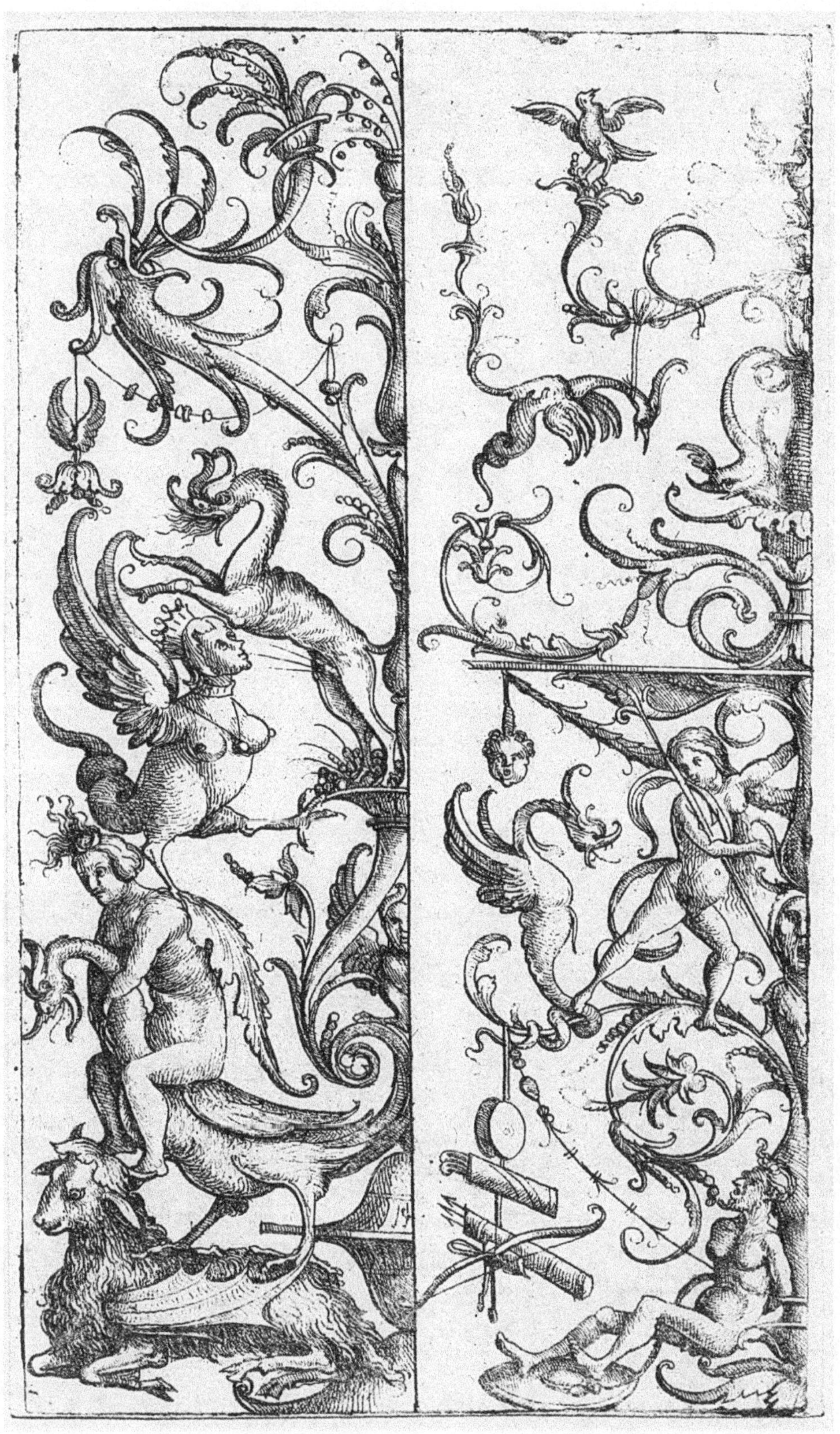

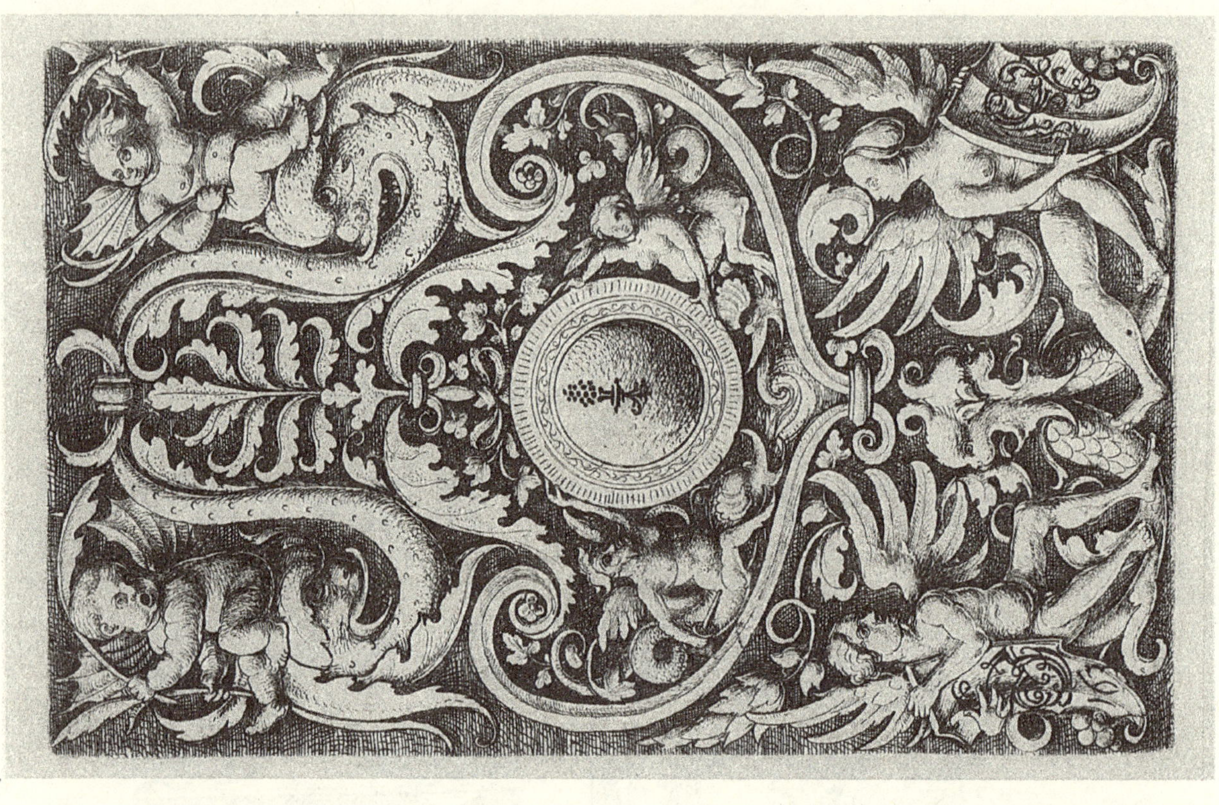

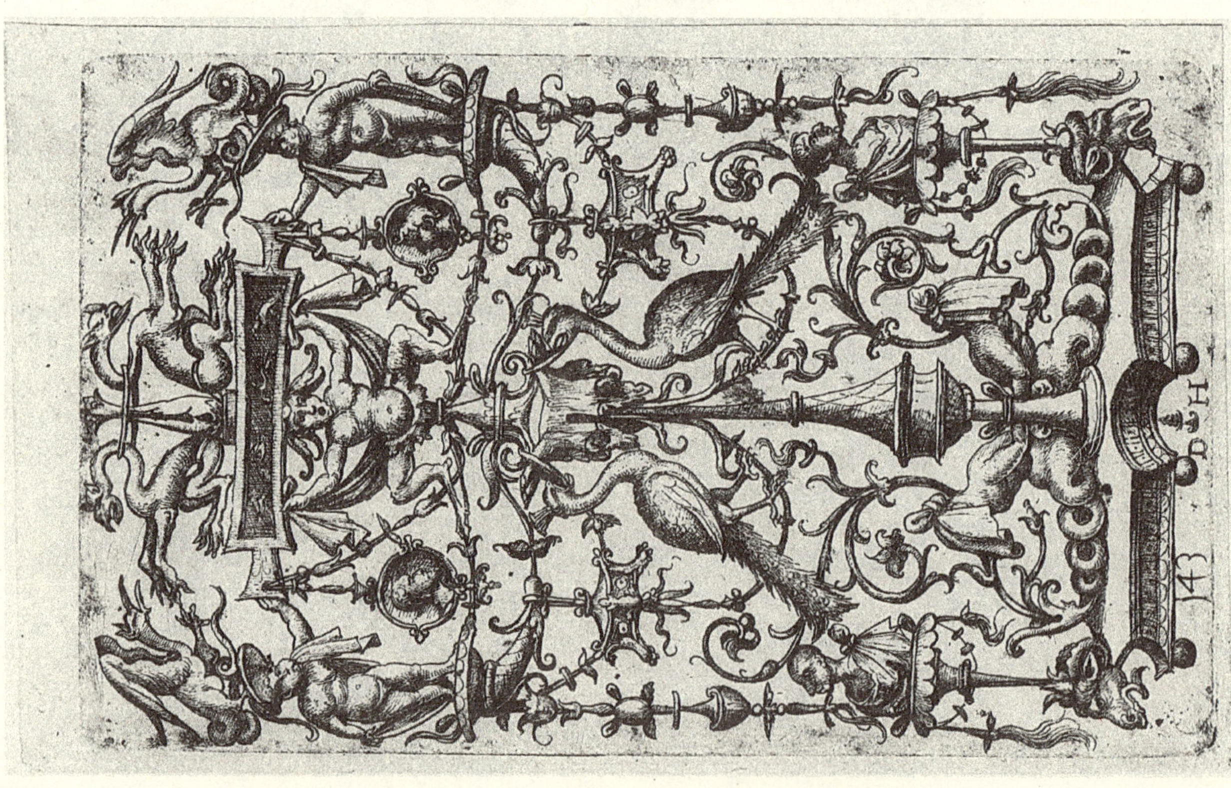

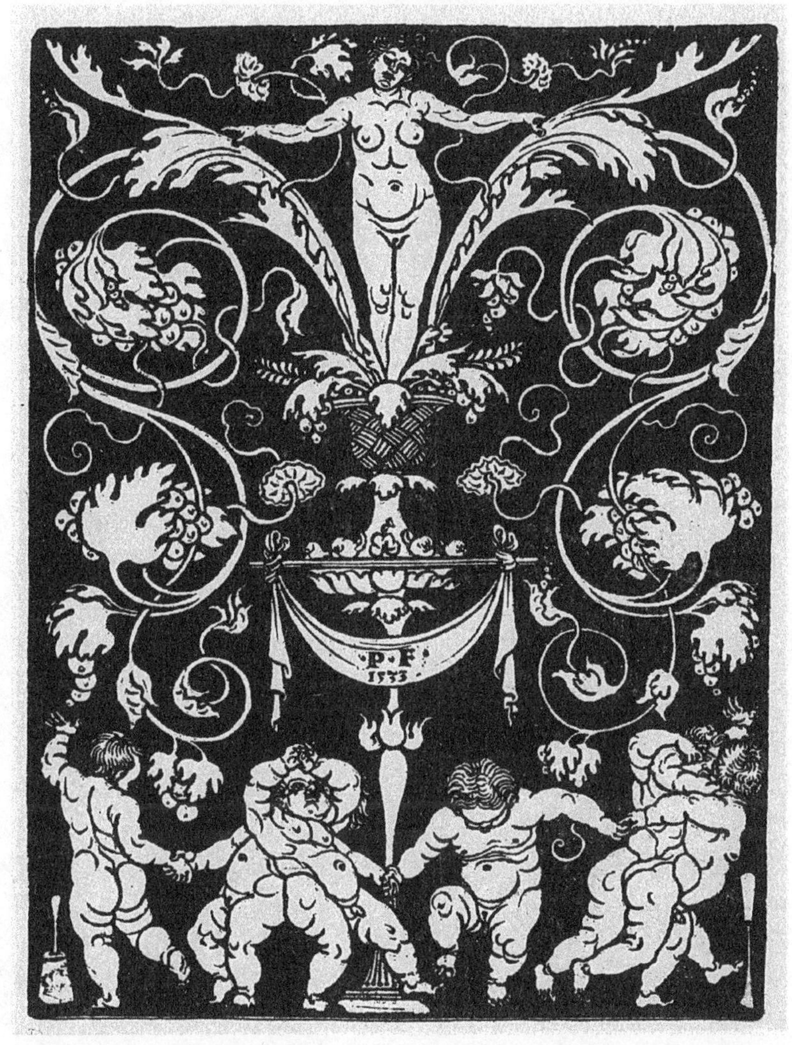
P·F
1533

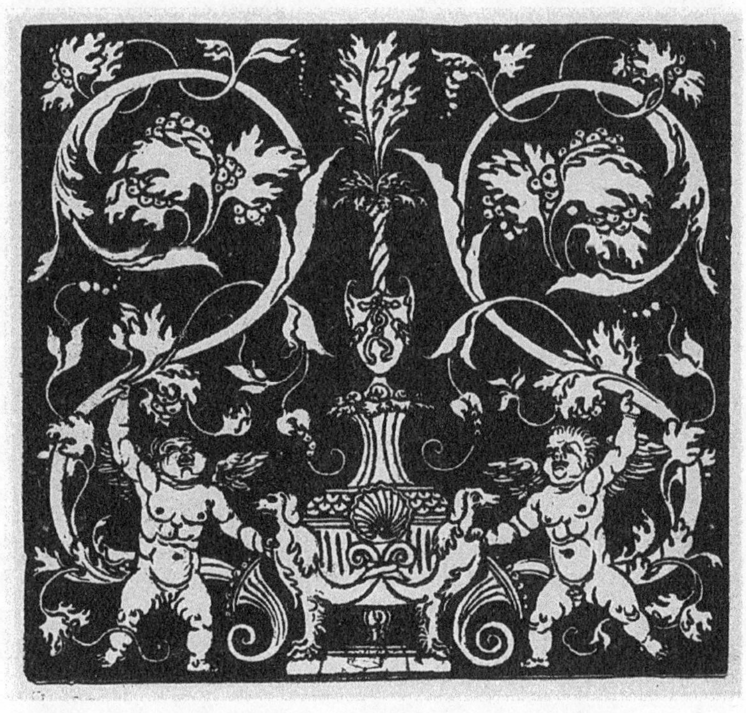

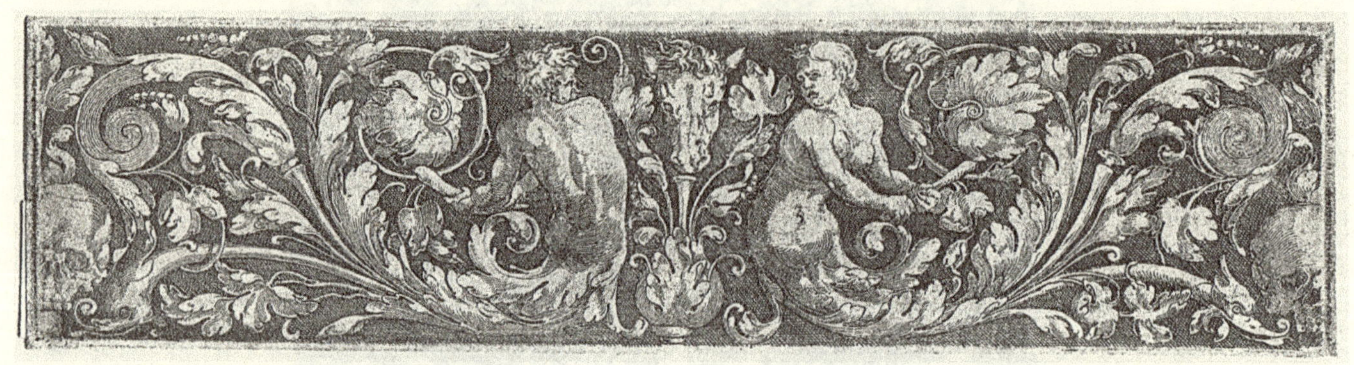

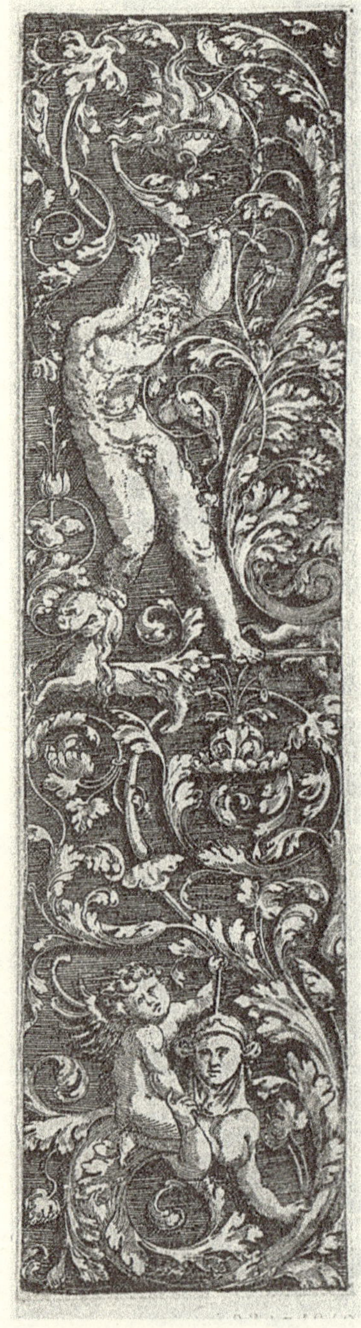

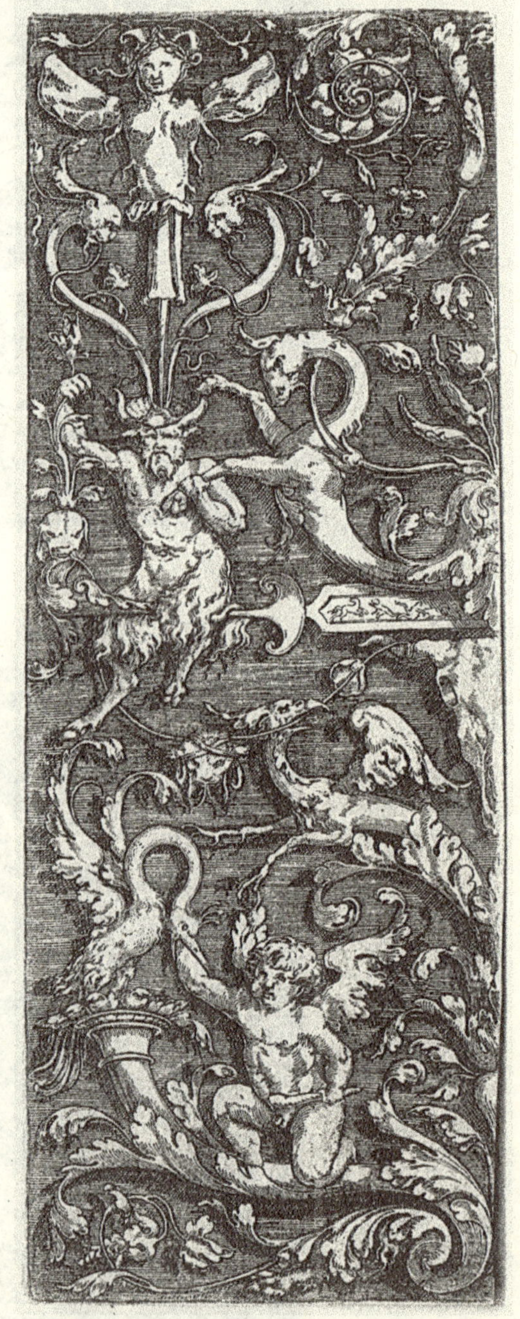

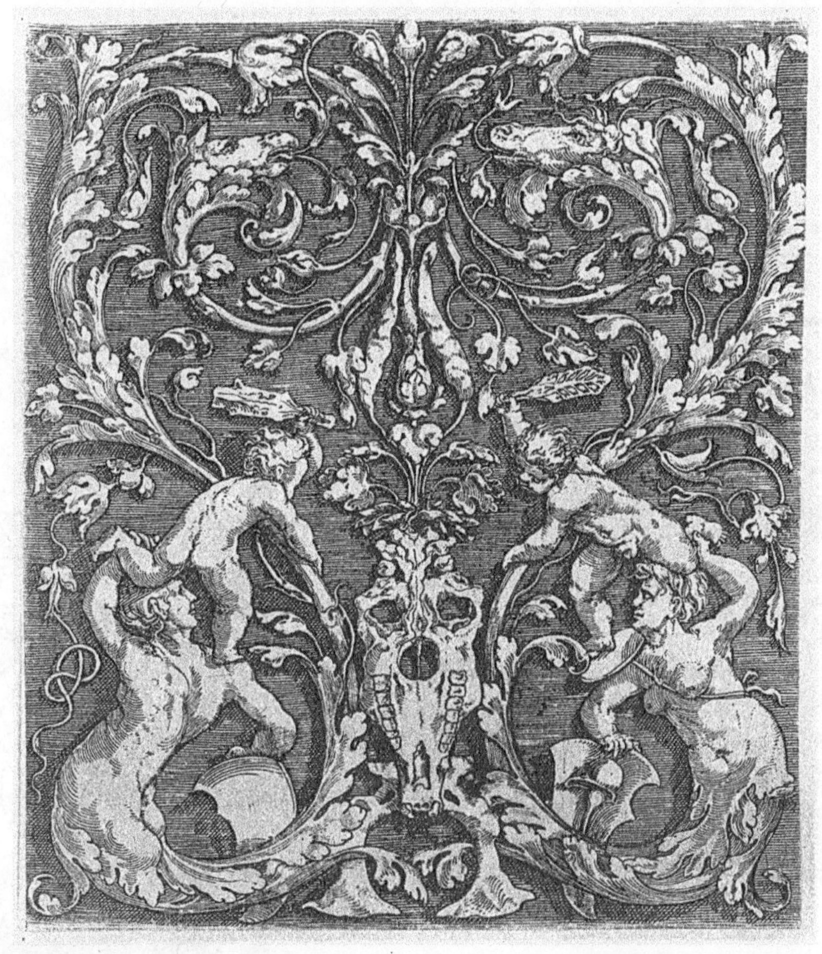

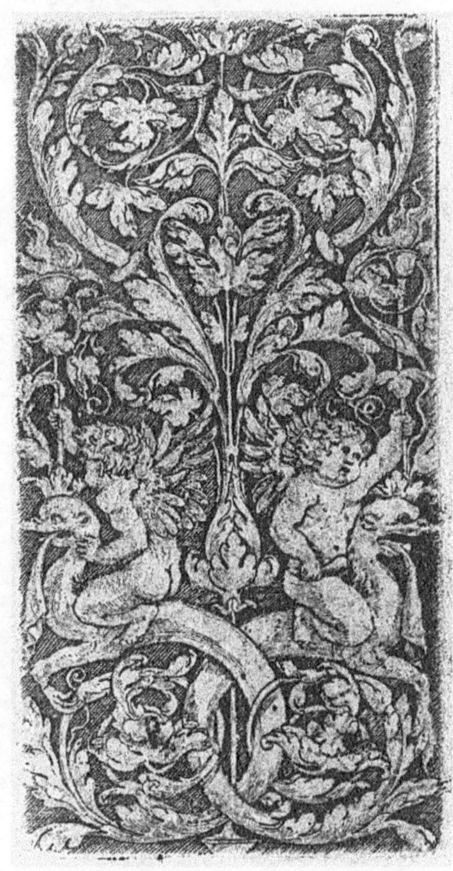

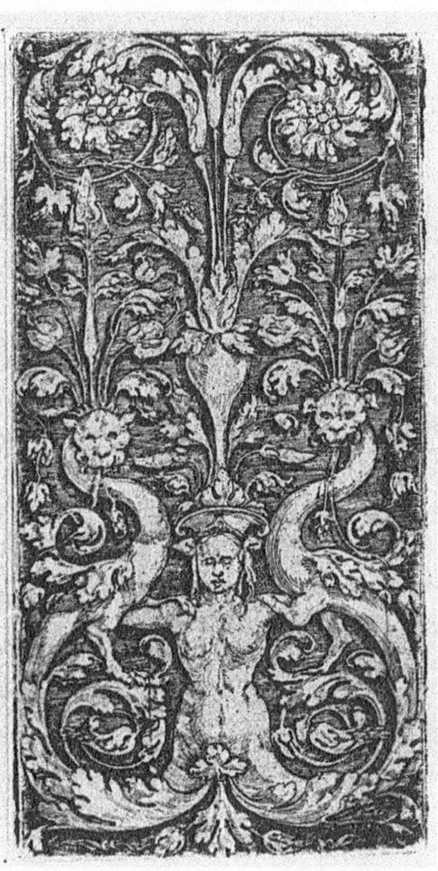

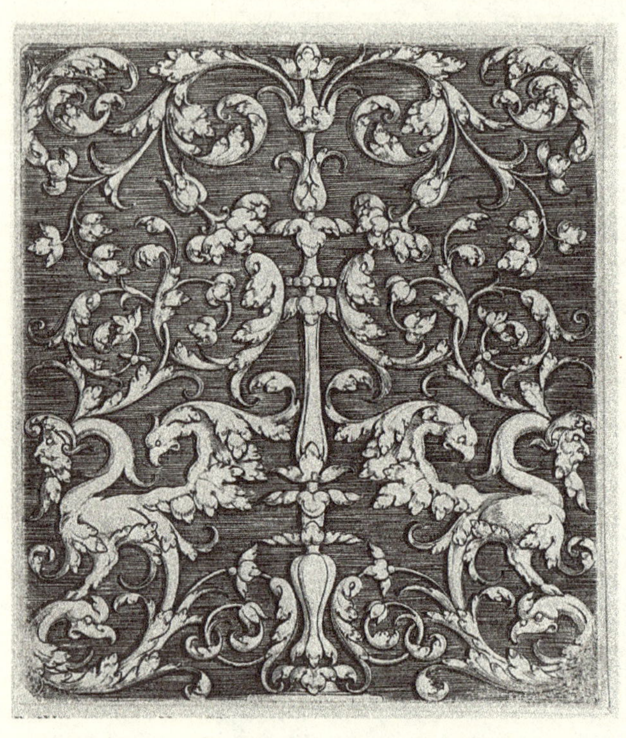

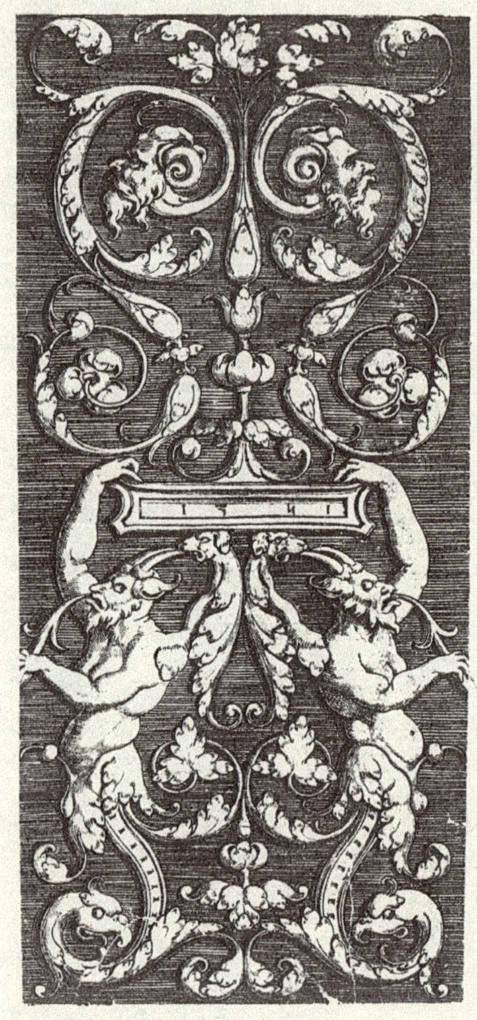

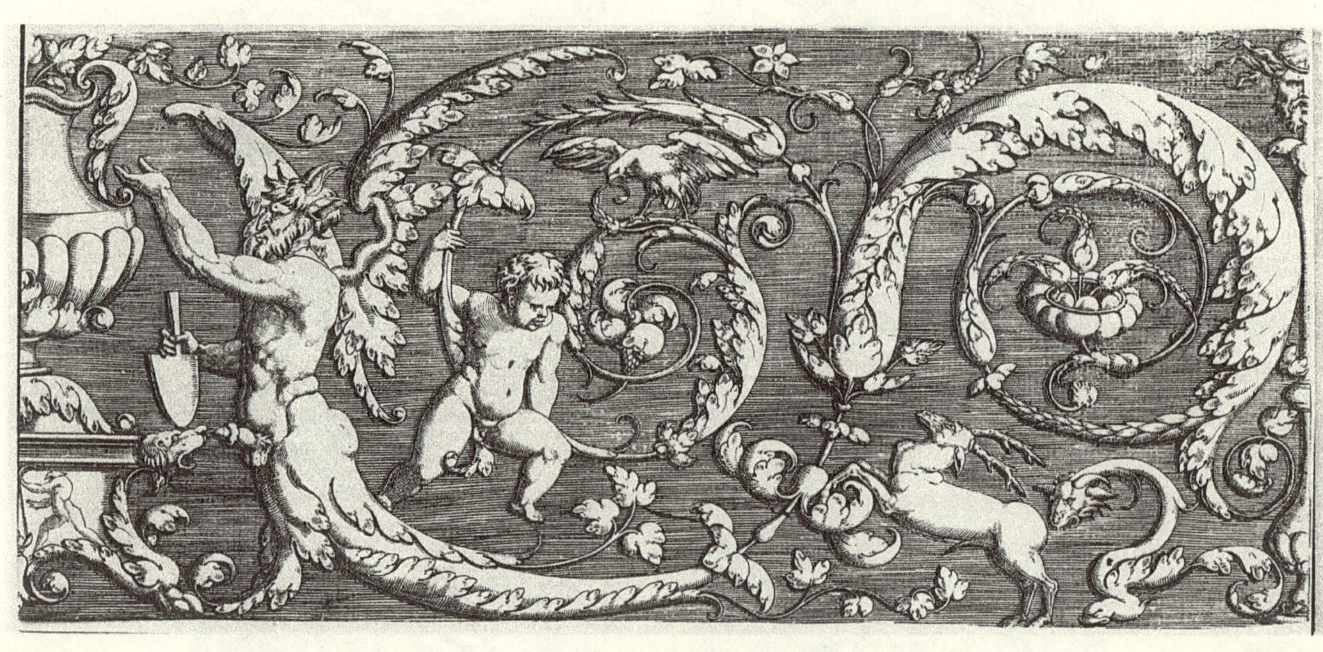

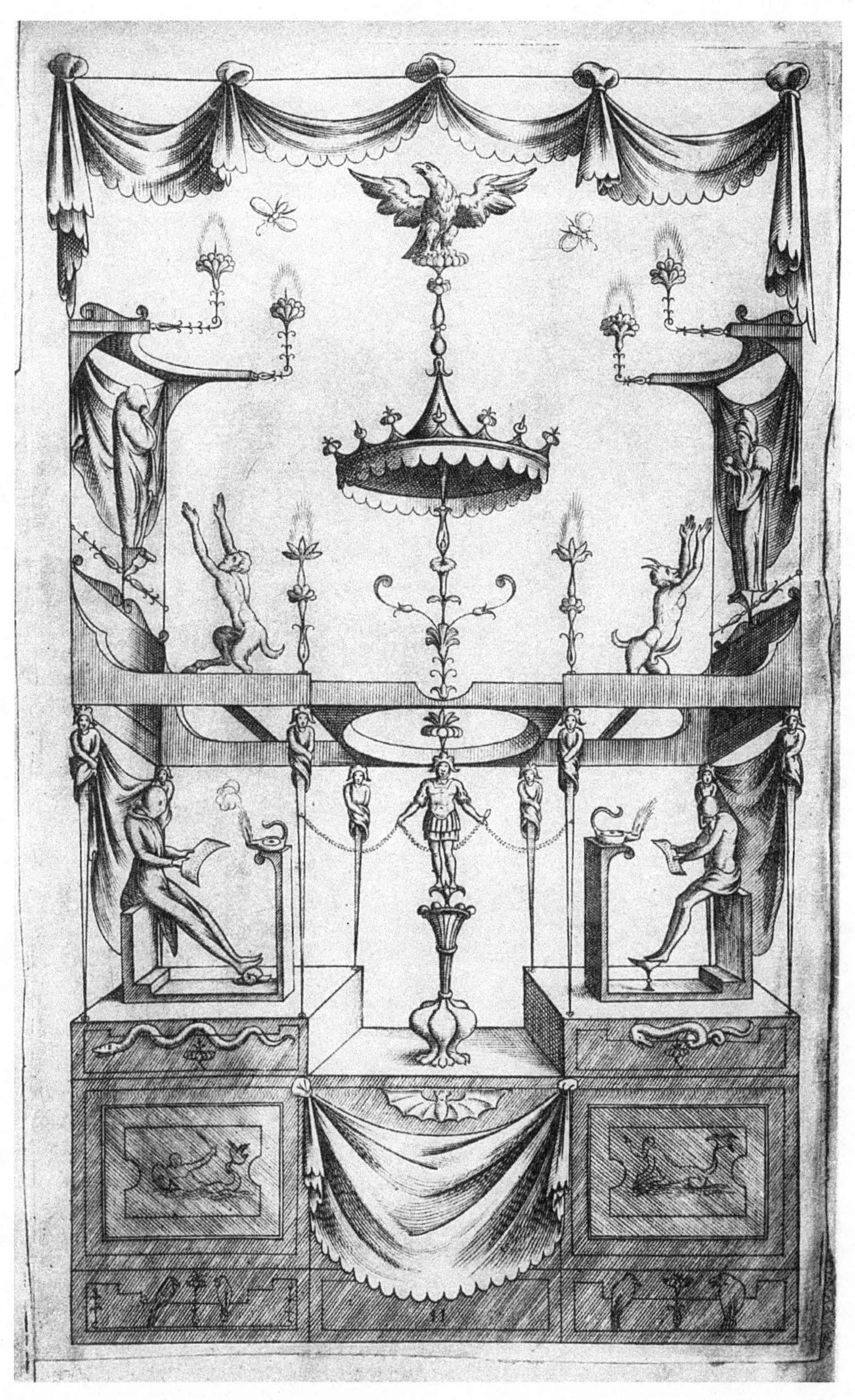

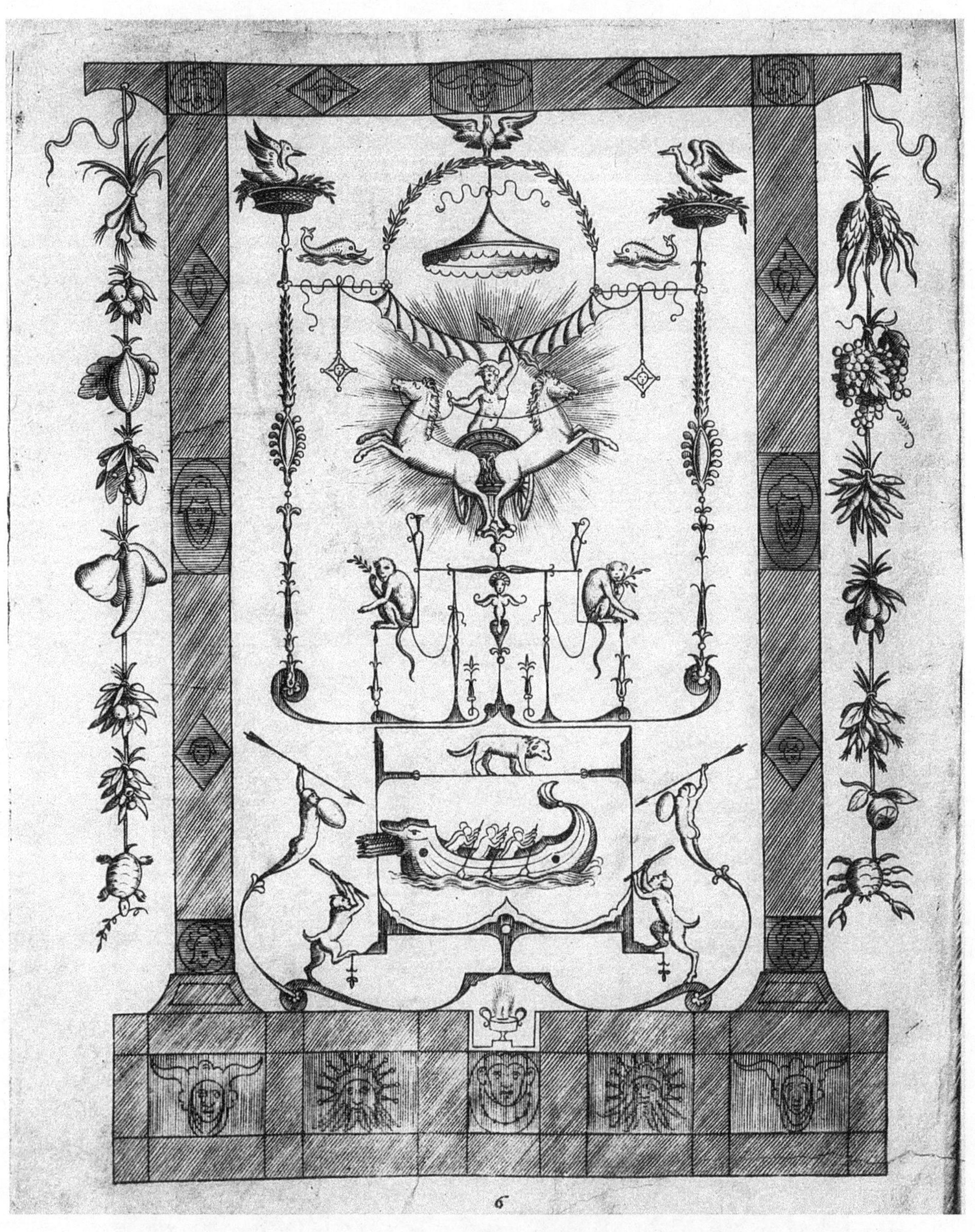

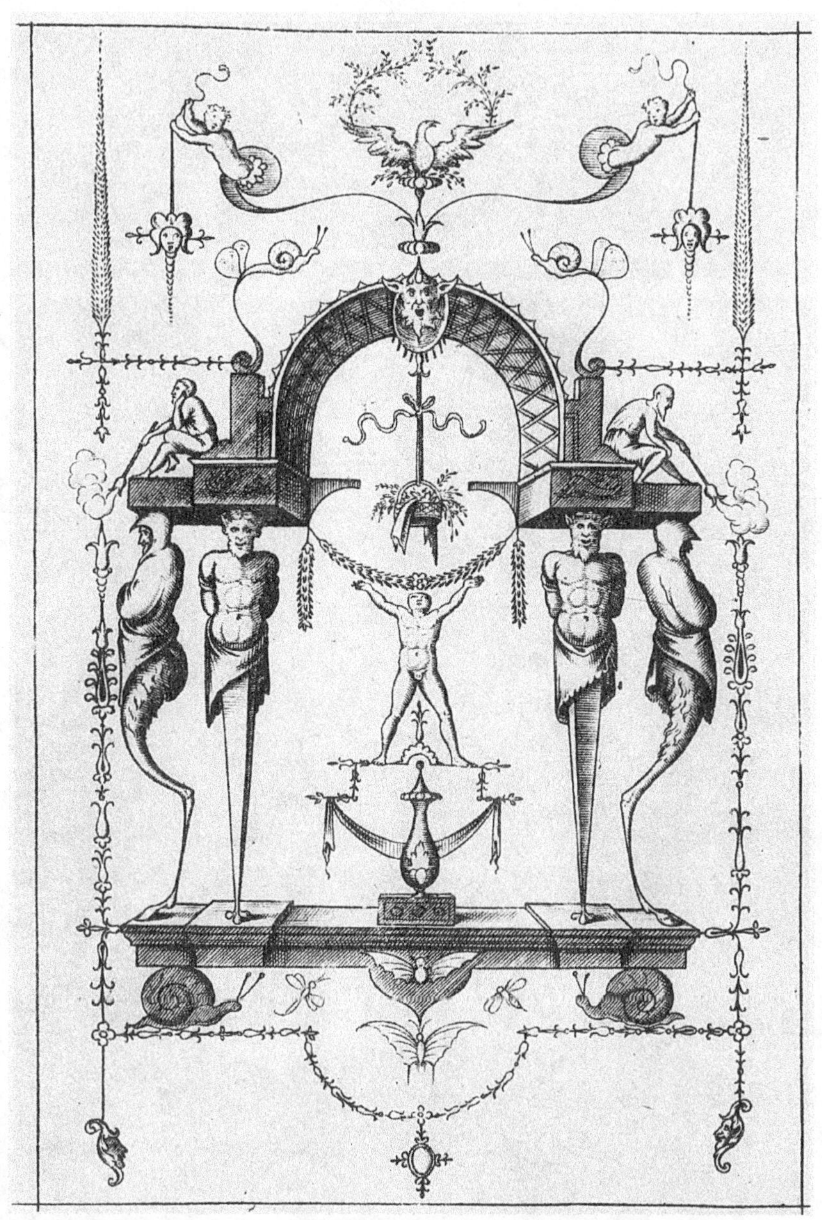

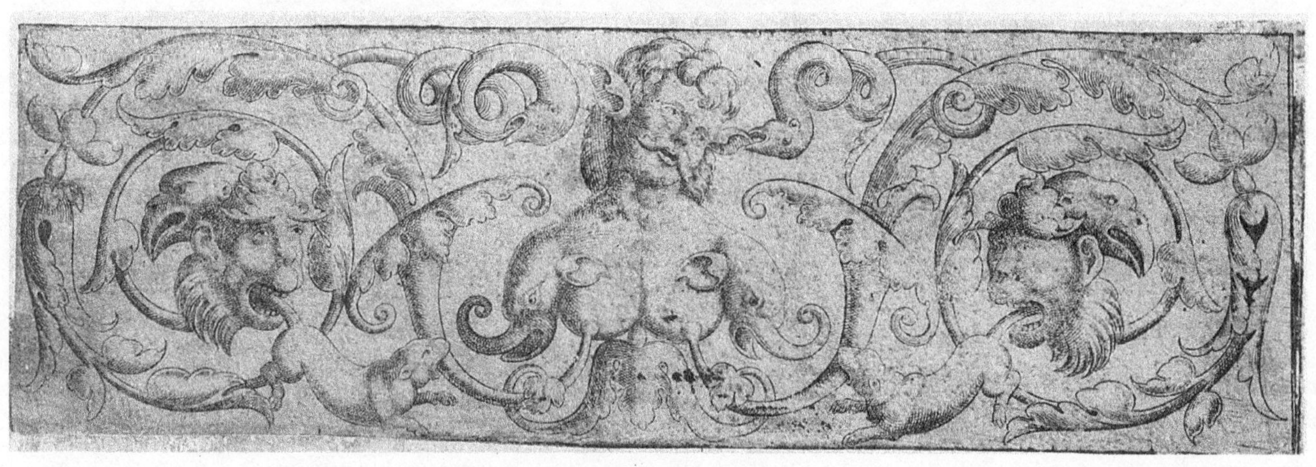

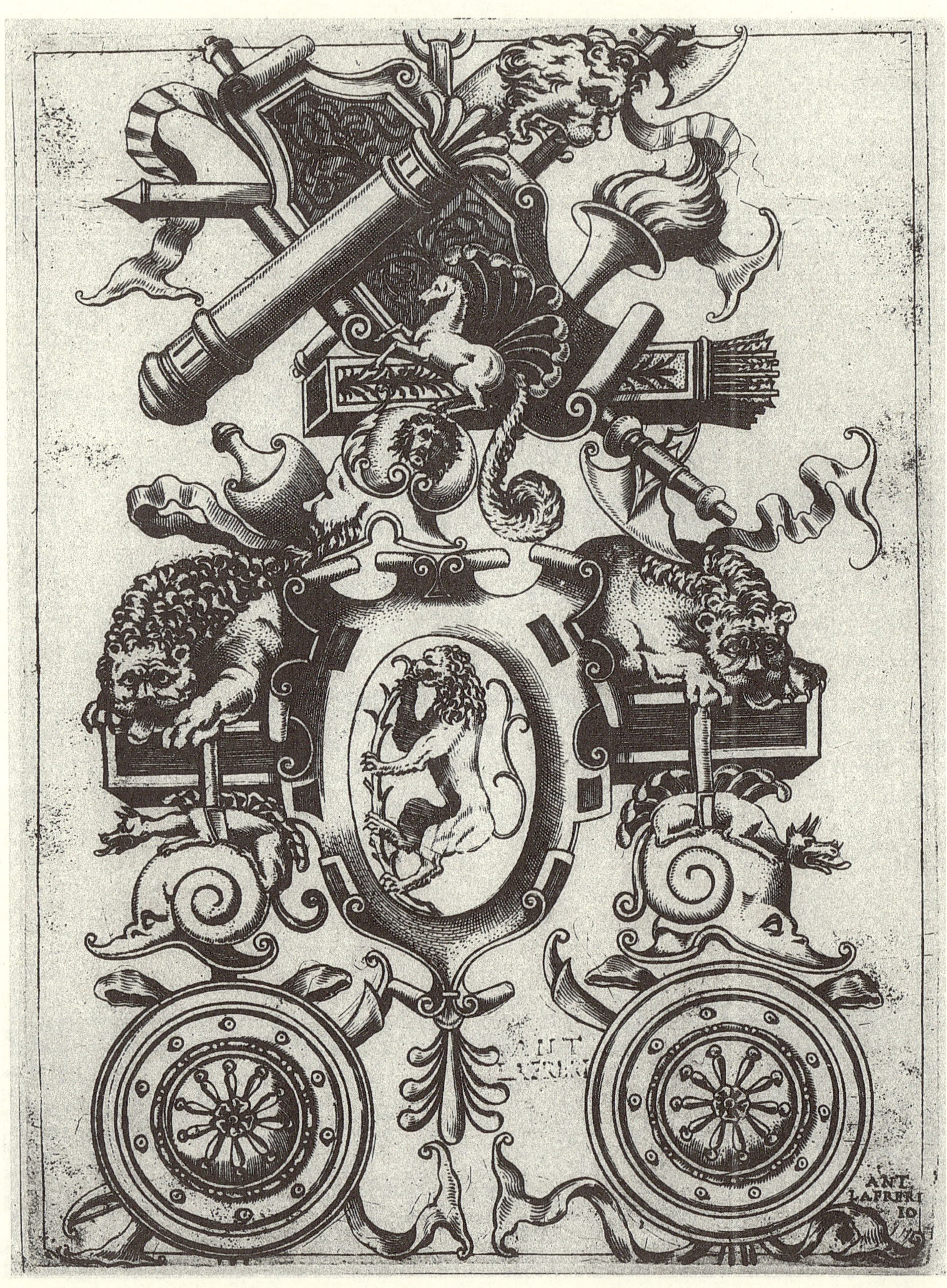
ANT.
LAFRERI
IO

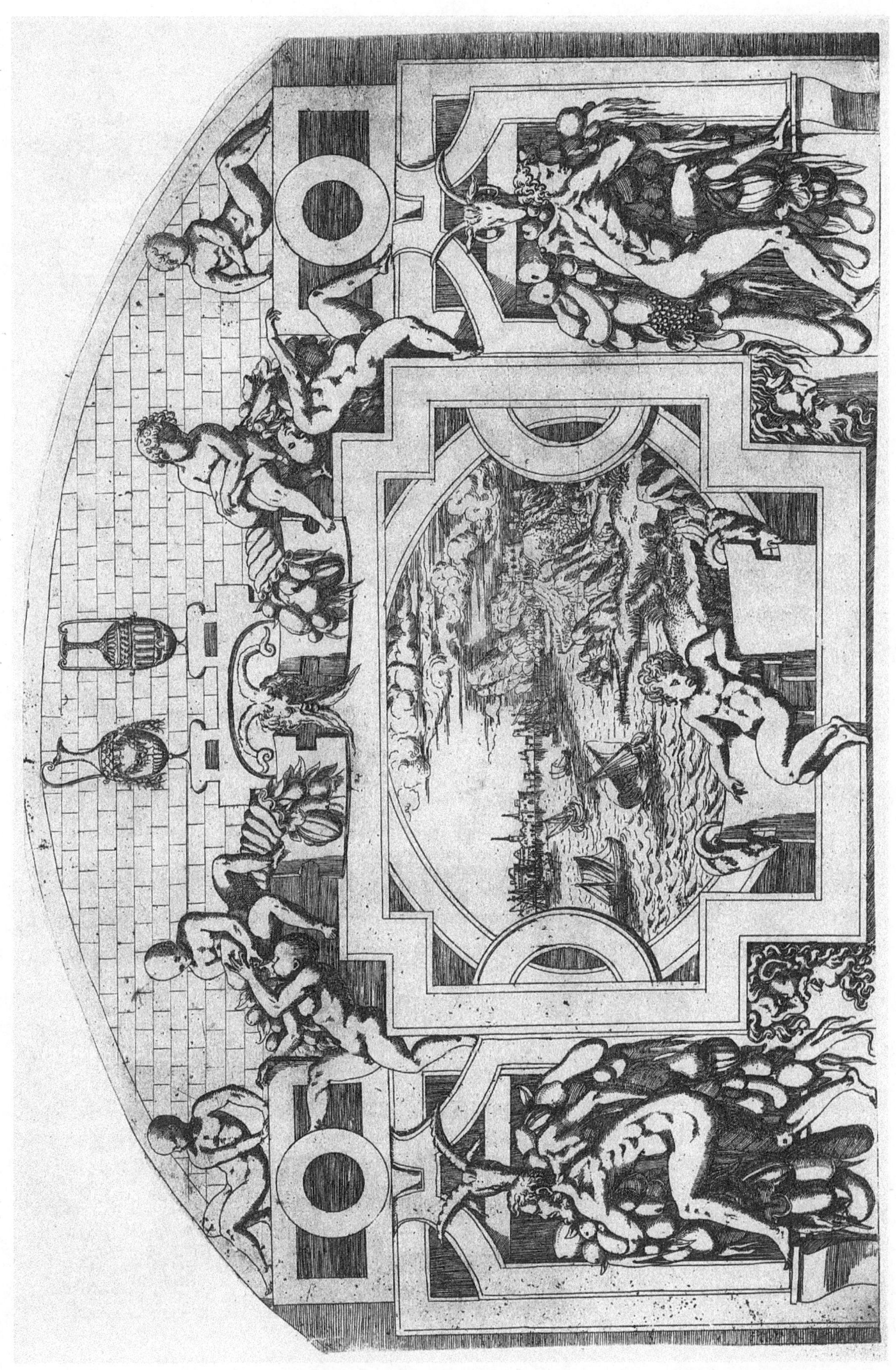

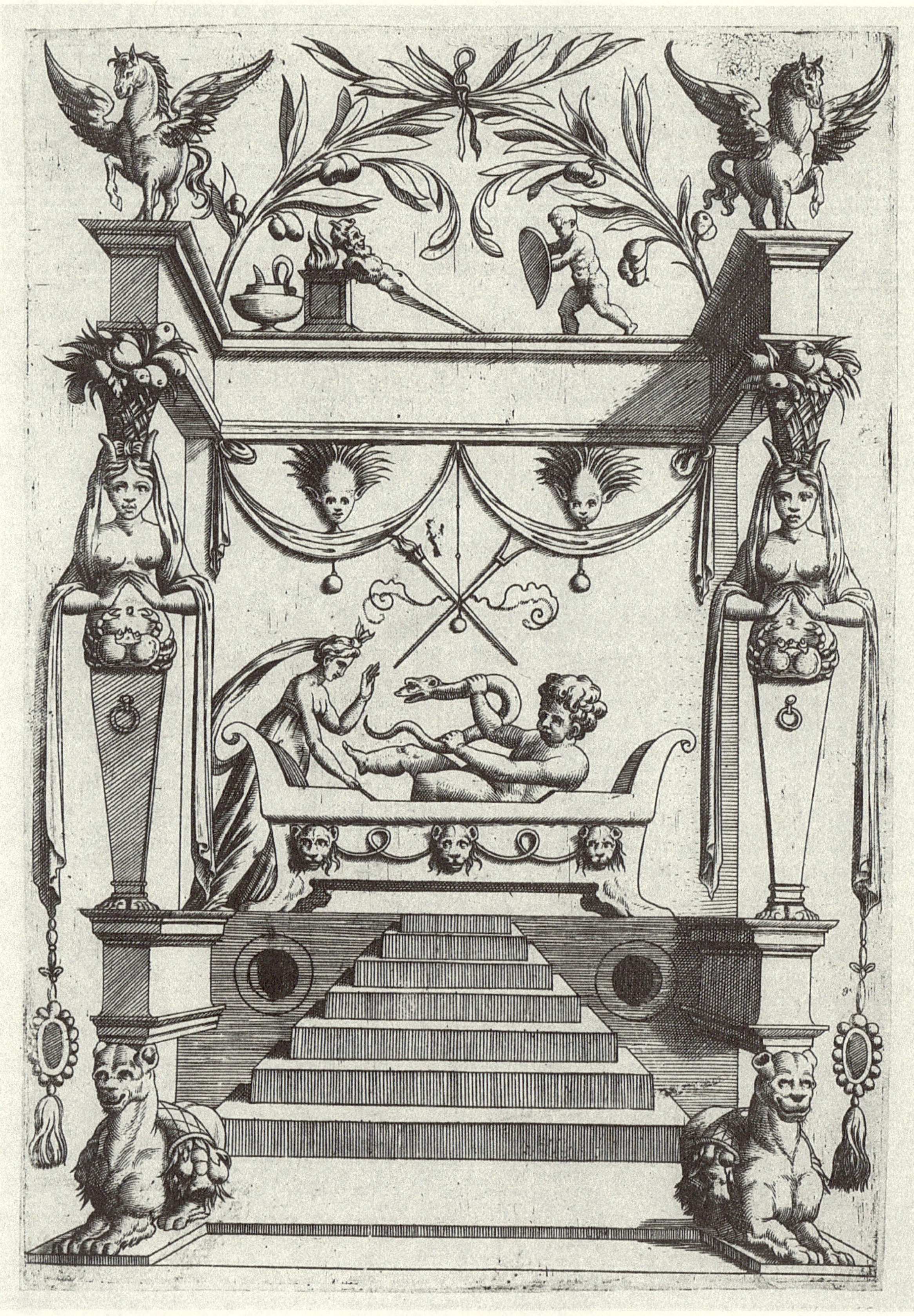

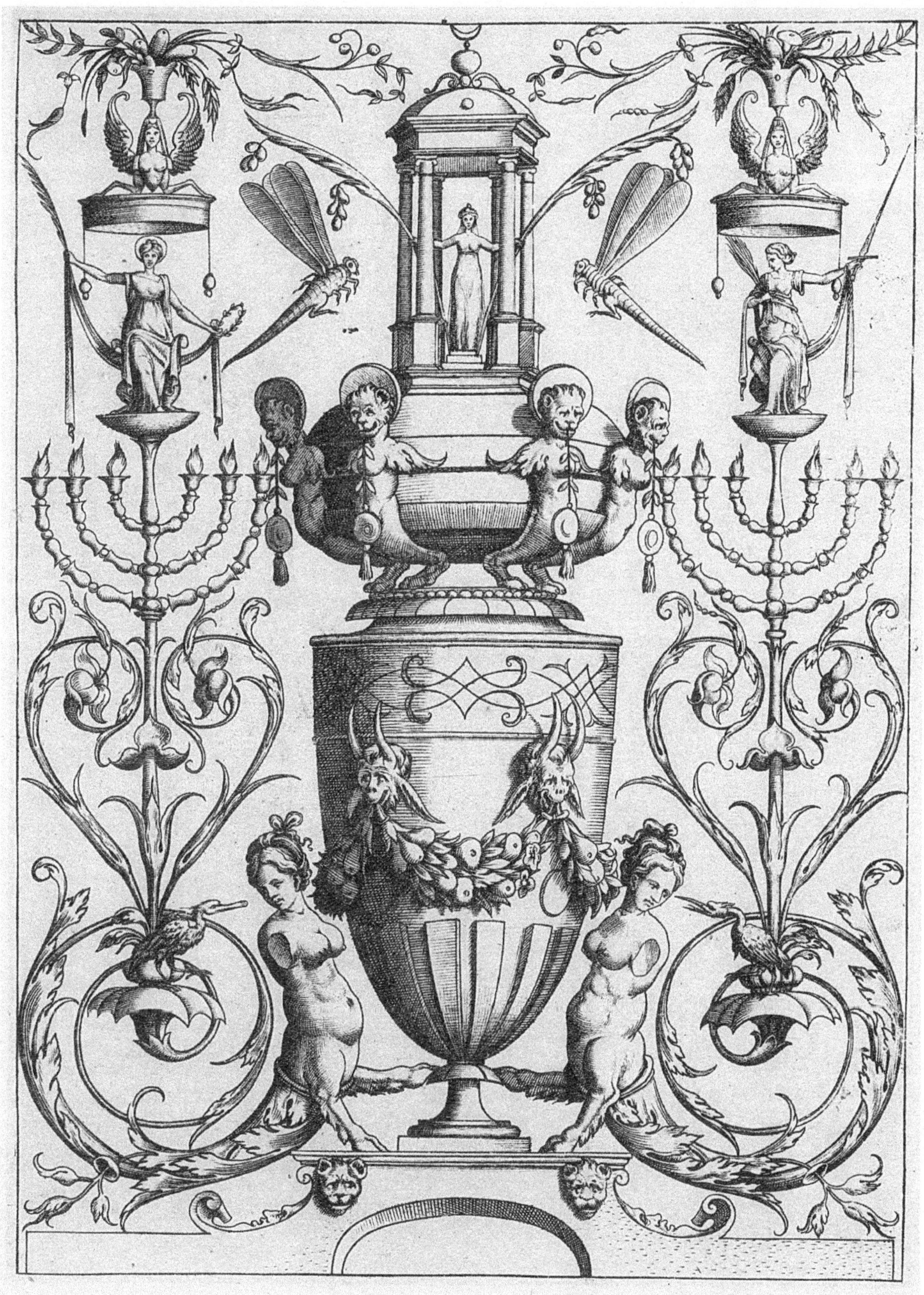

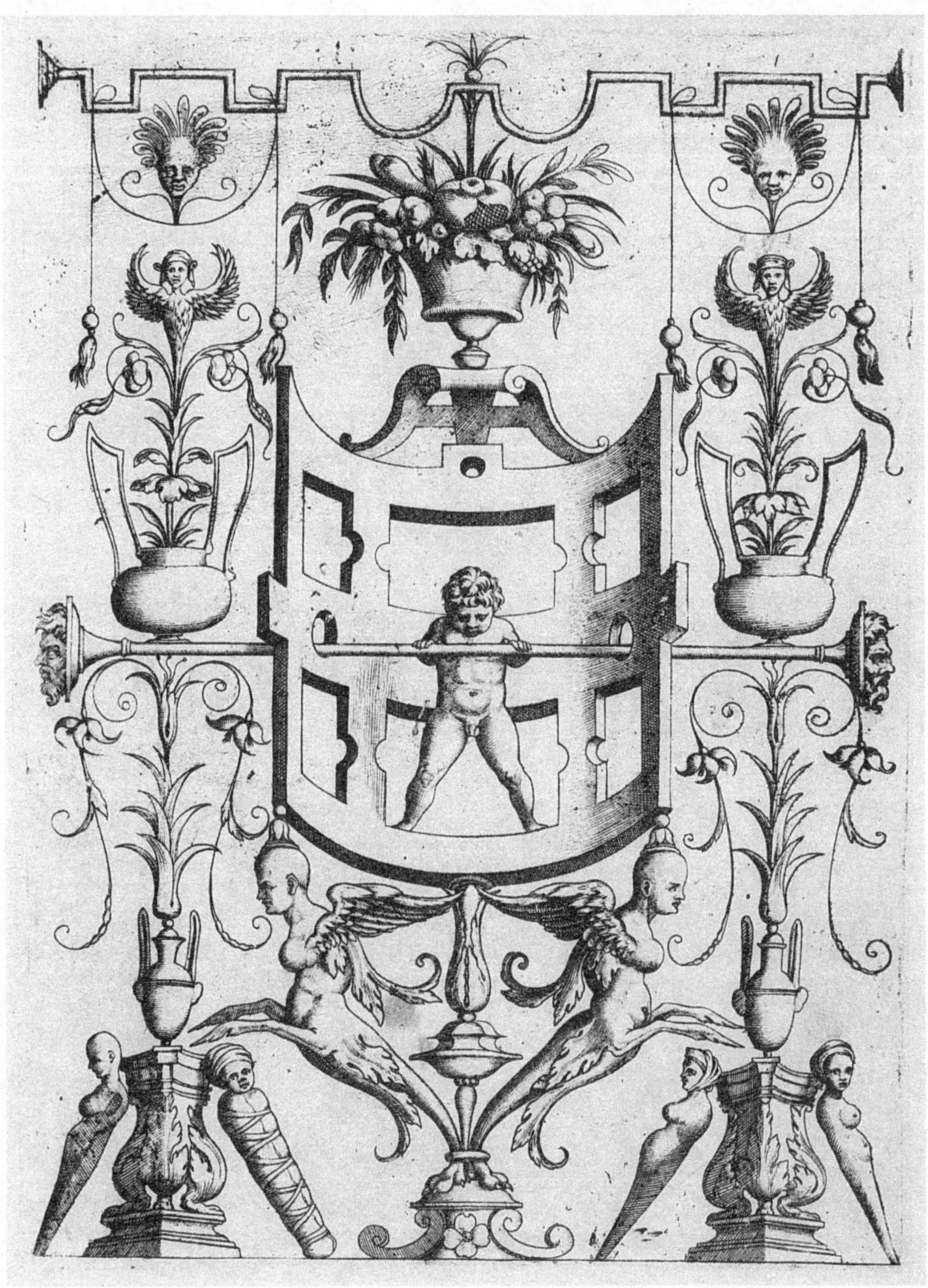

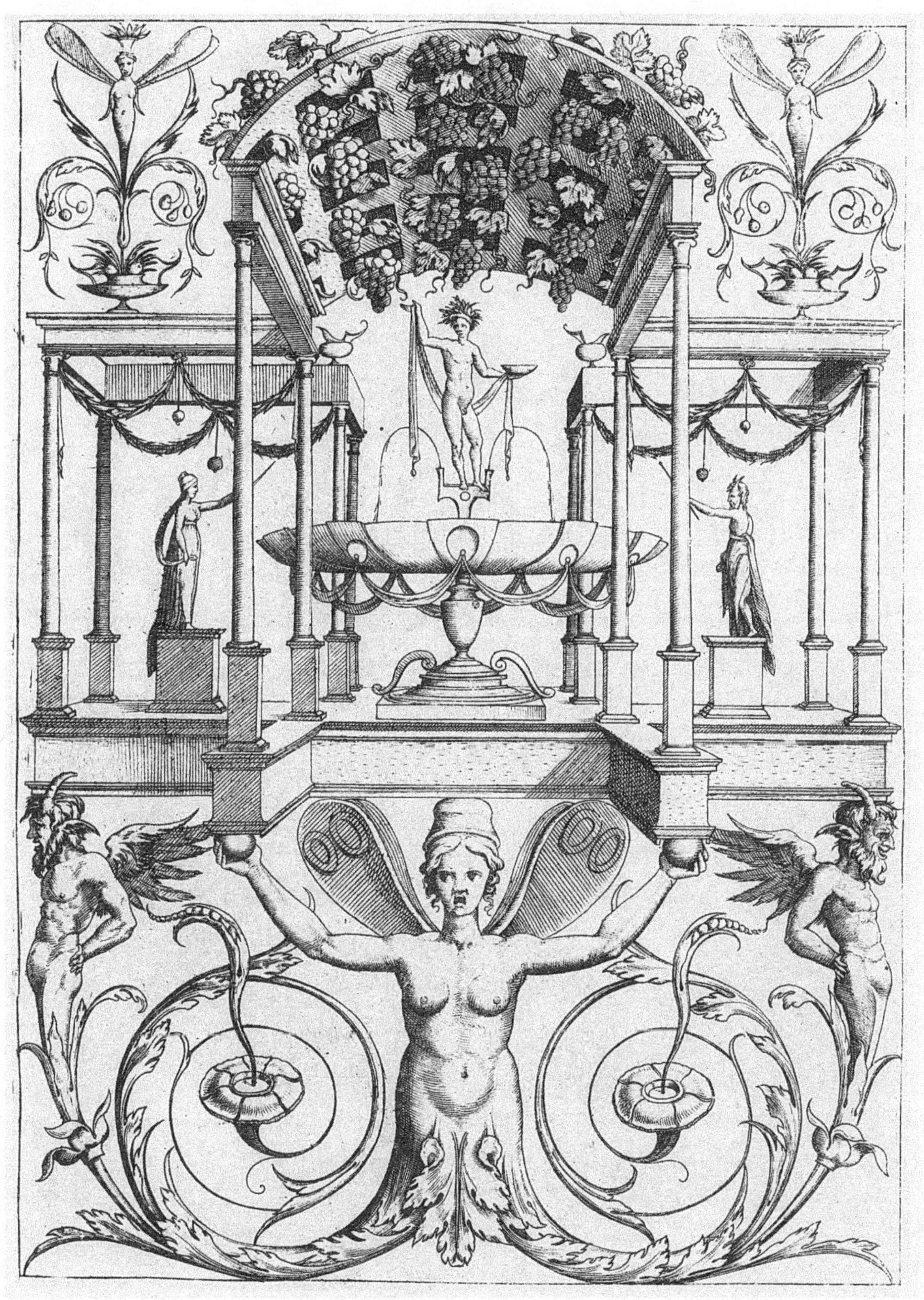

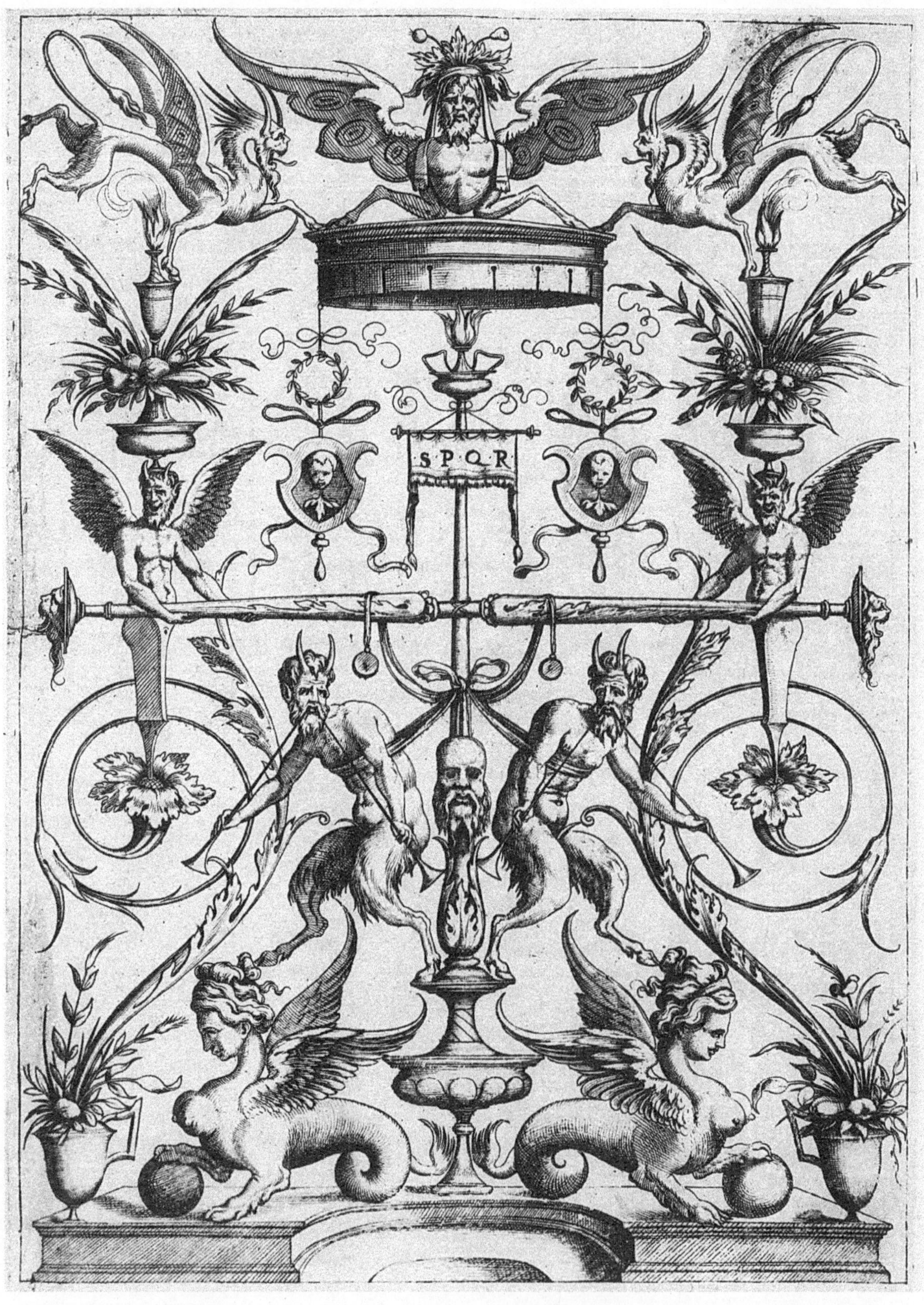
S.P.Q.R

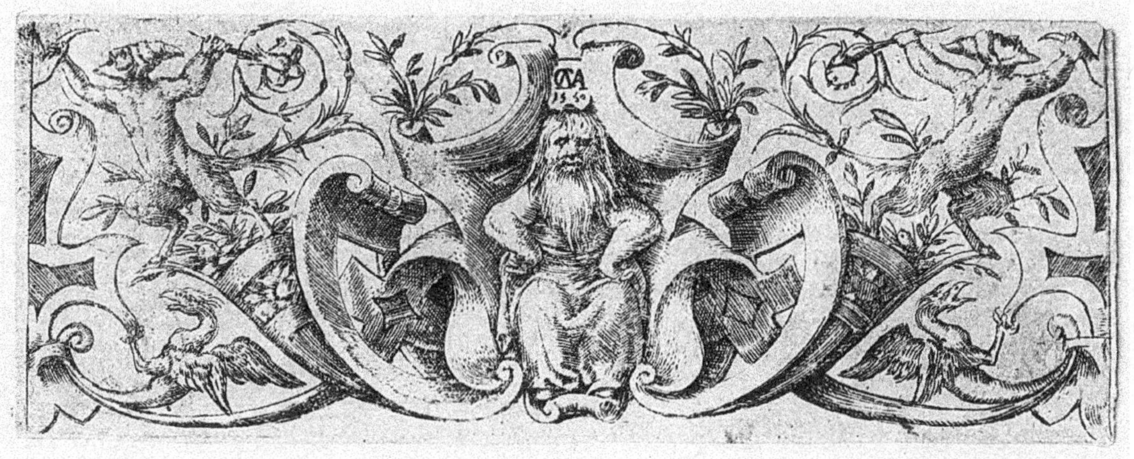

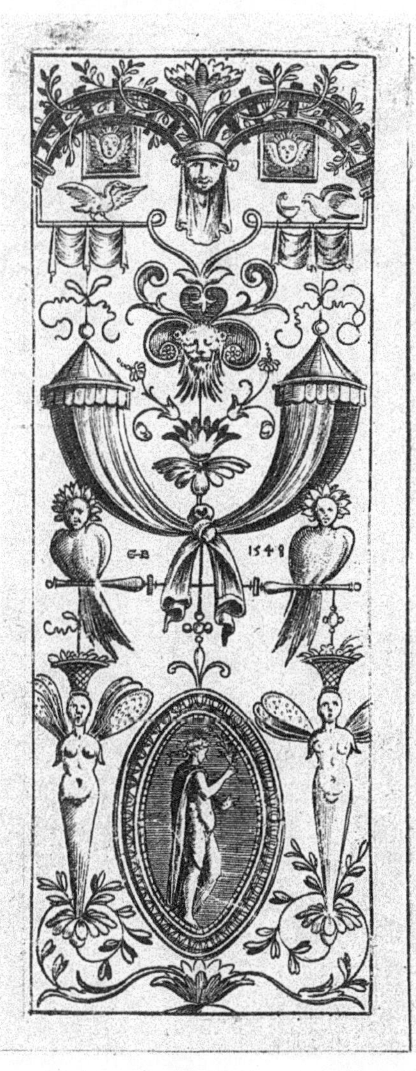
G·B
1548

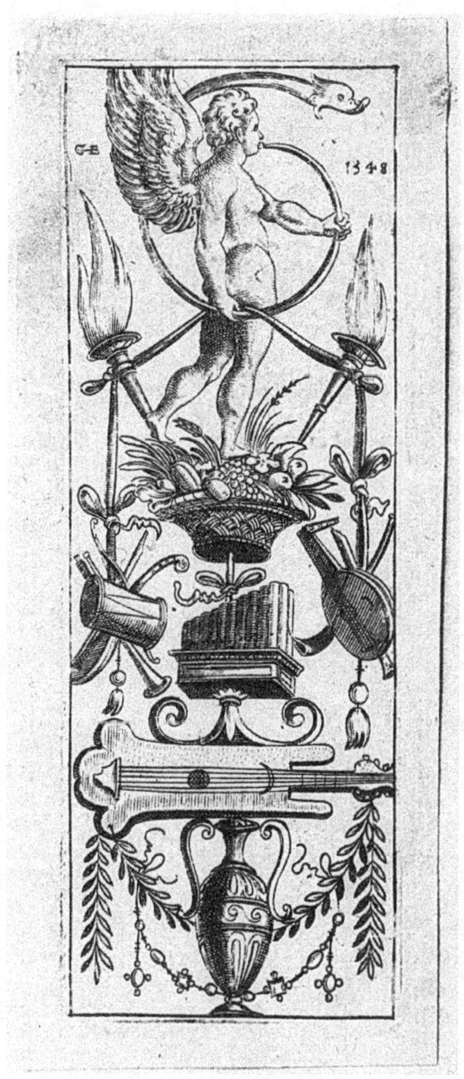
G·B
1548

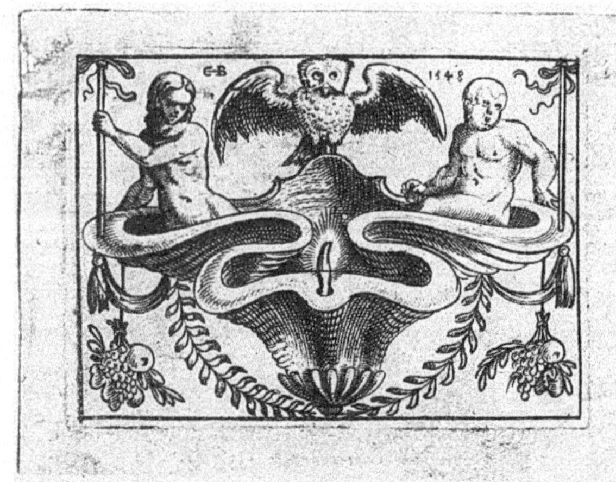

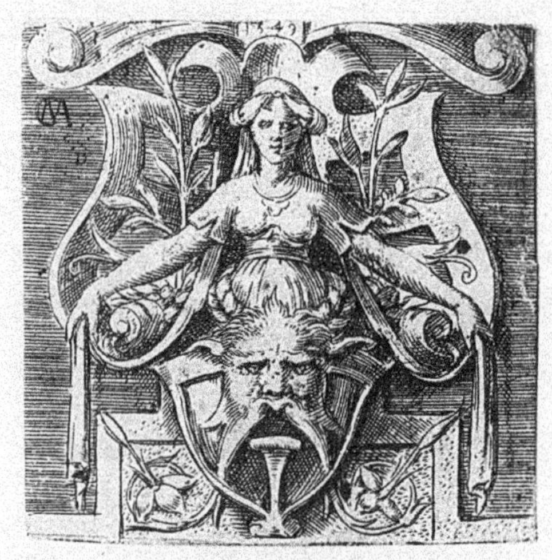

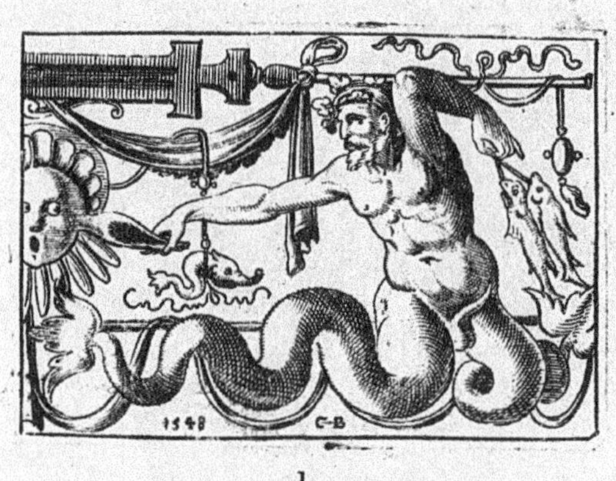

1

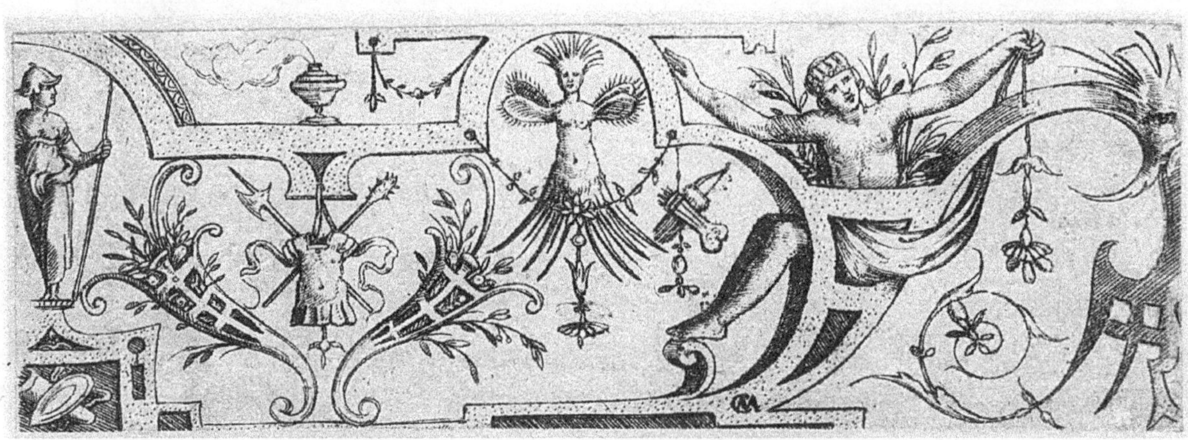

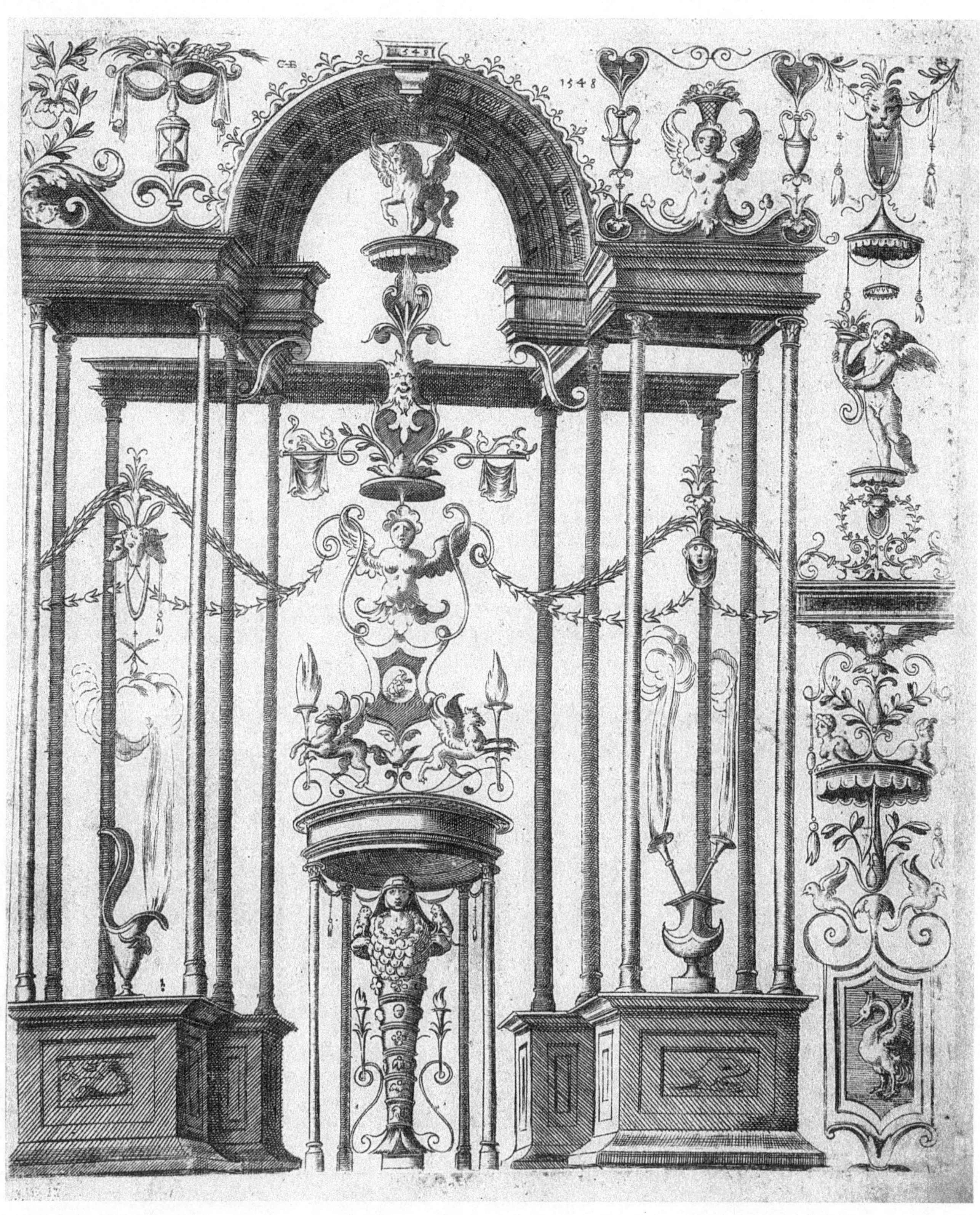

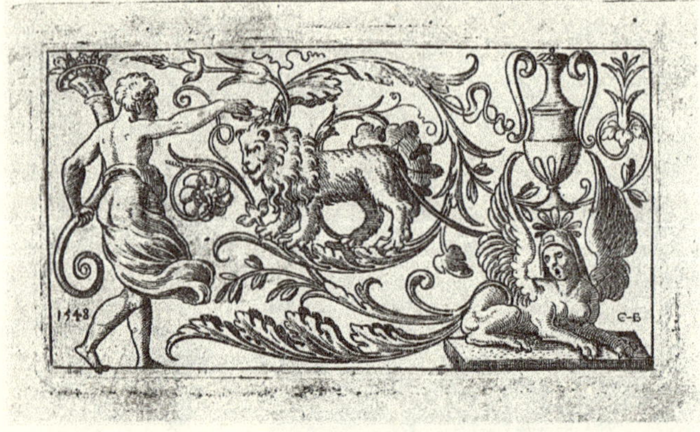
1548
C-B

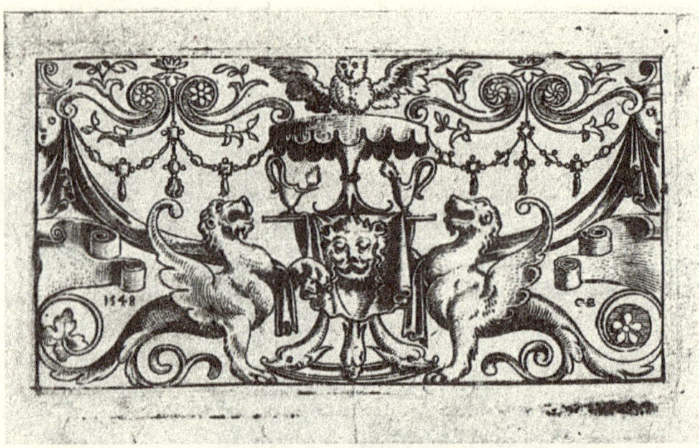
1548
CB

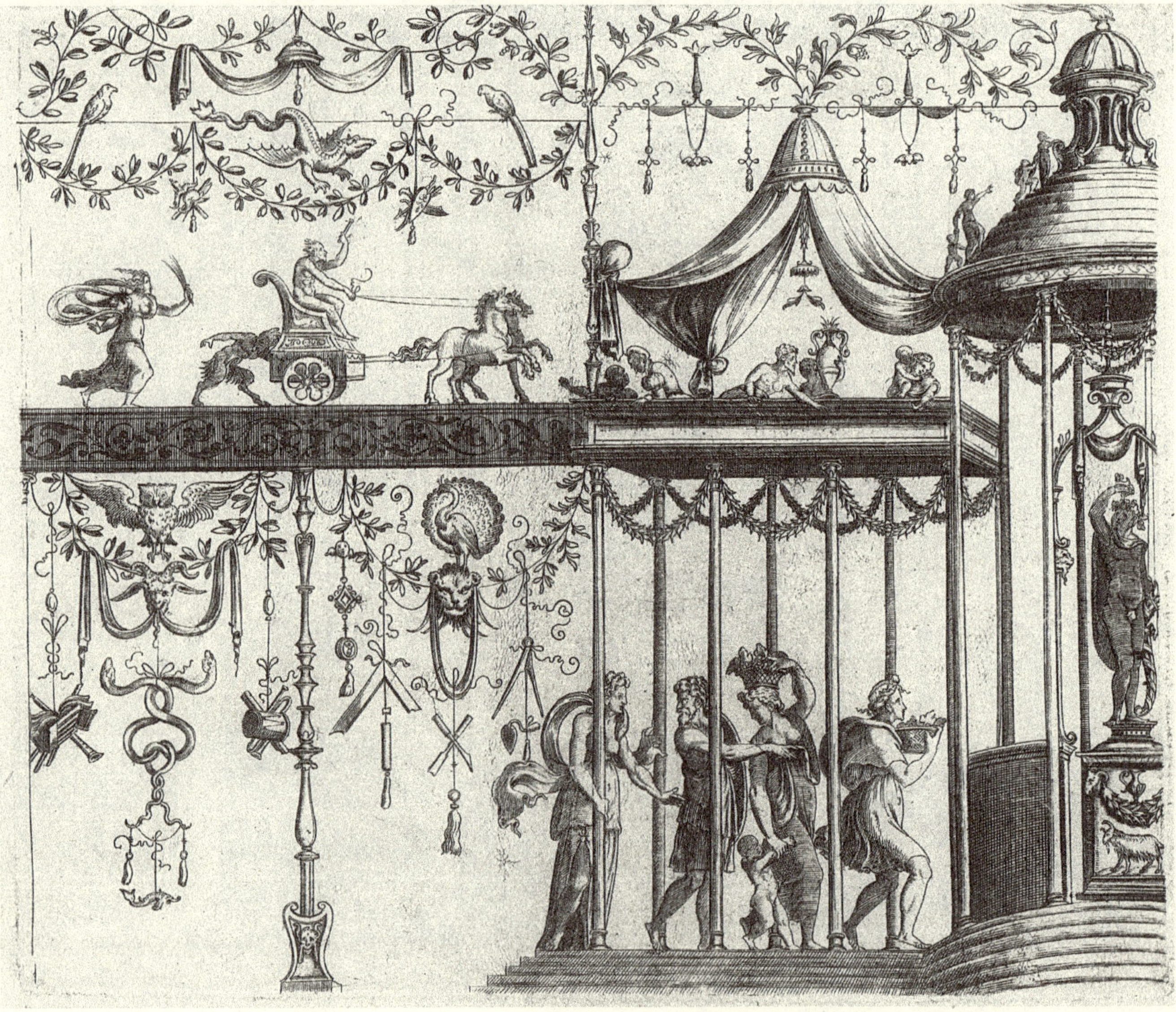

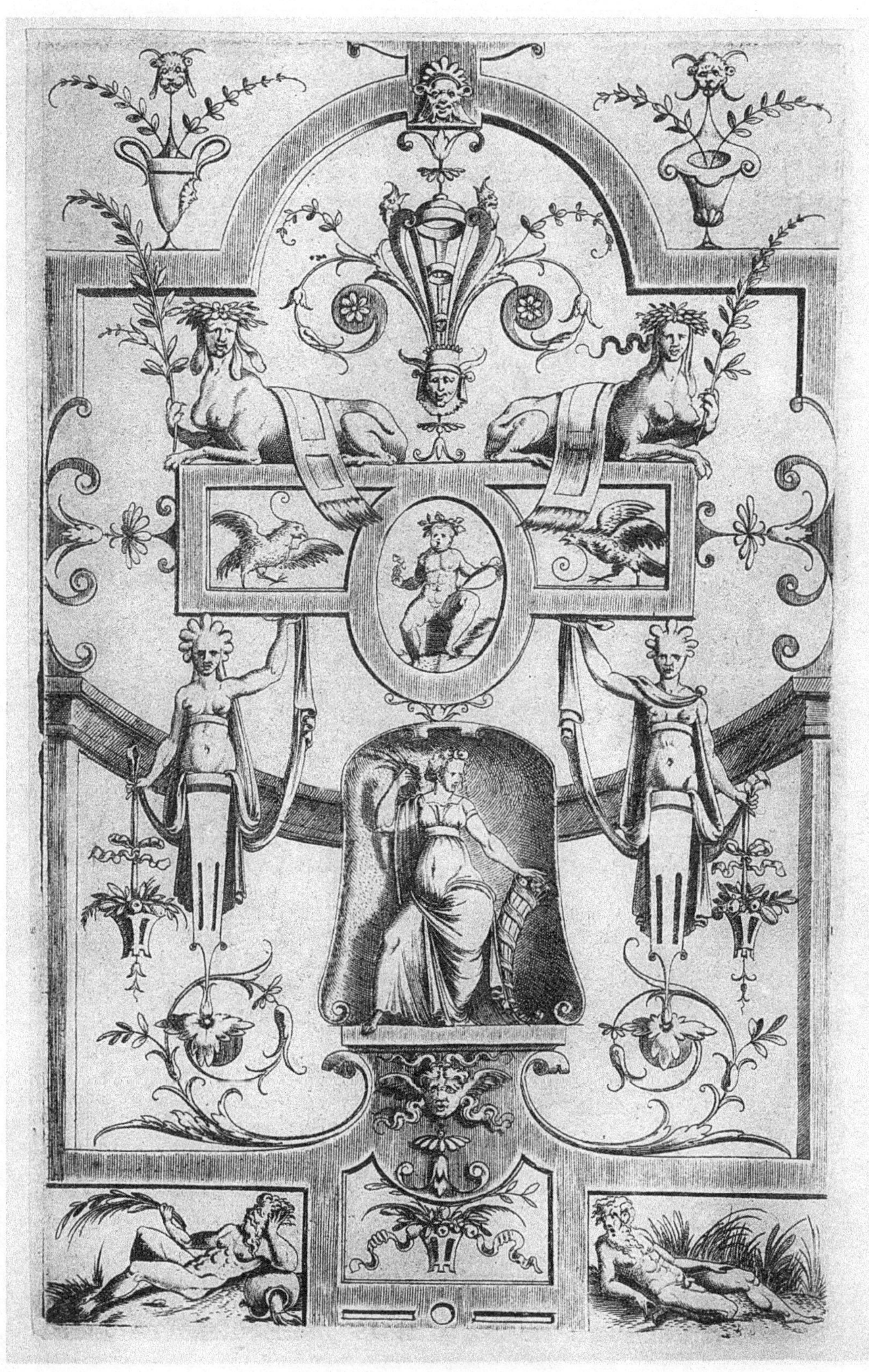

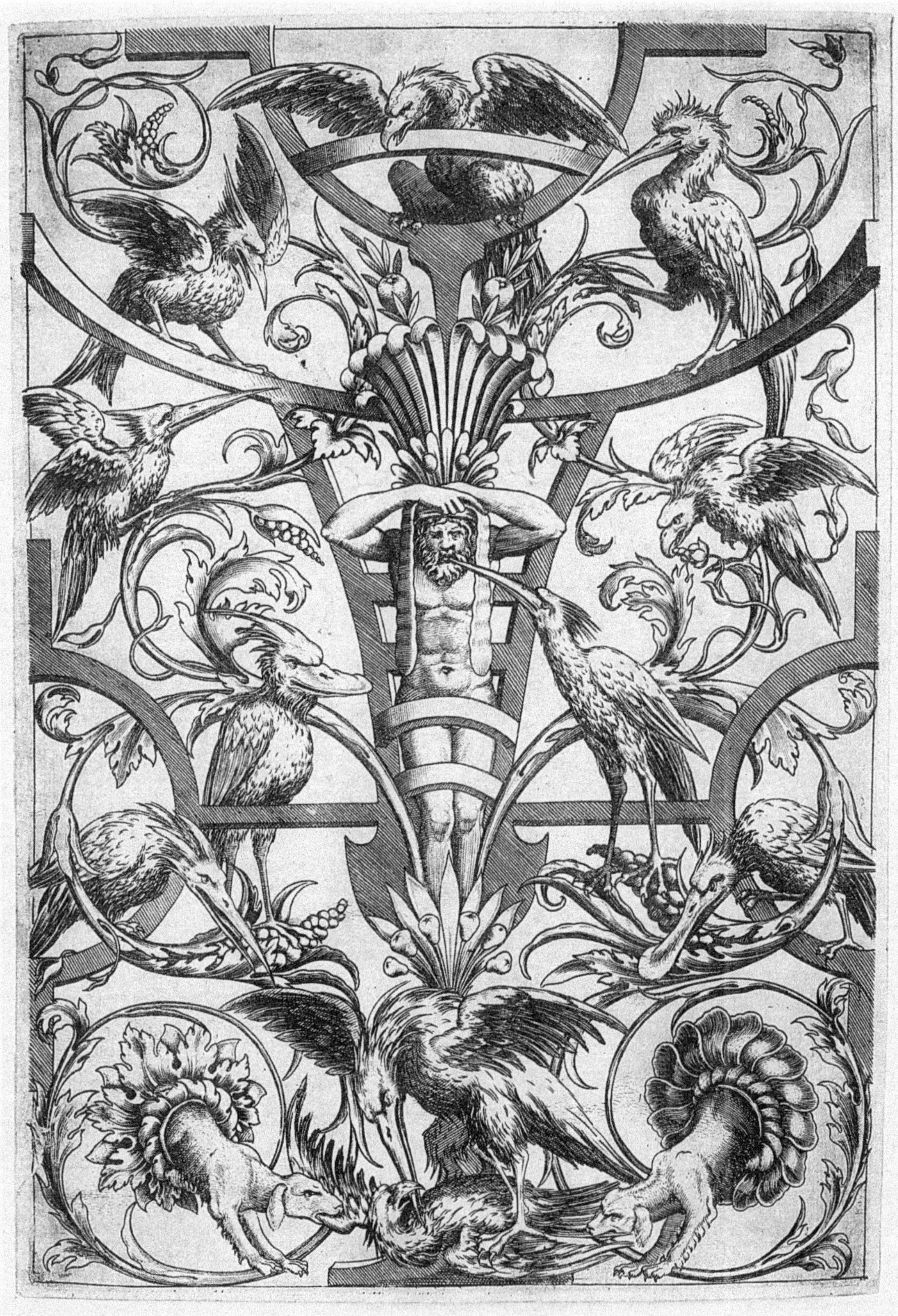

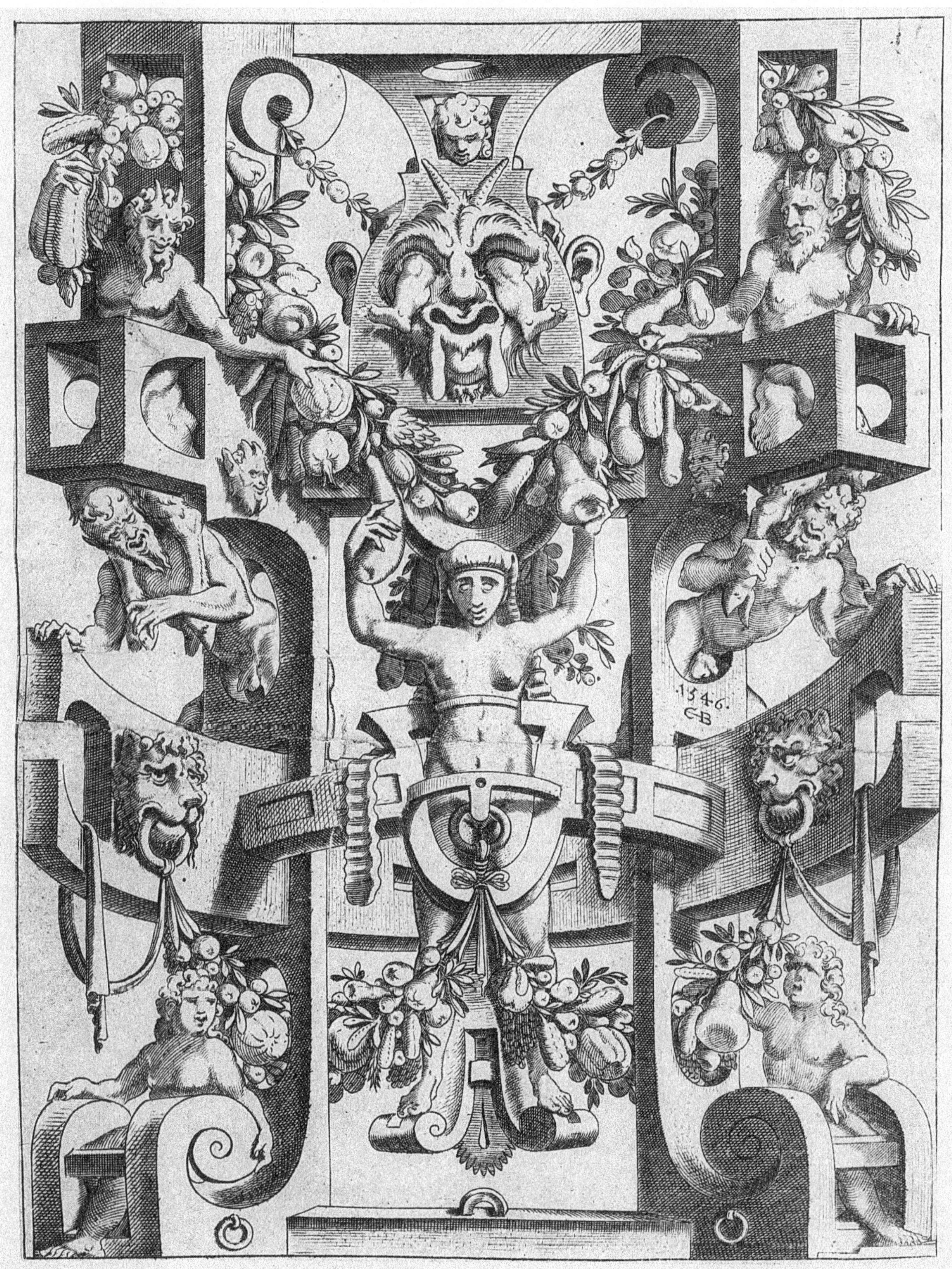
1546.
CB

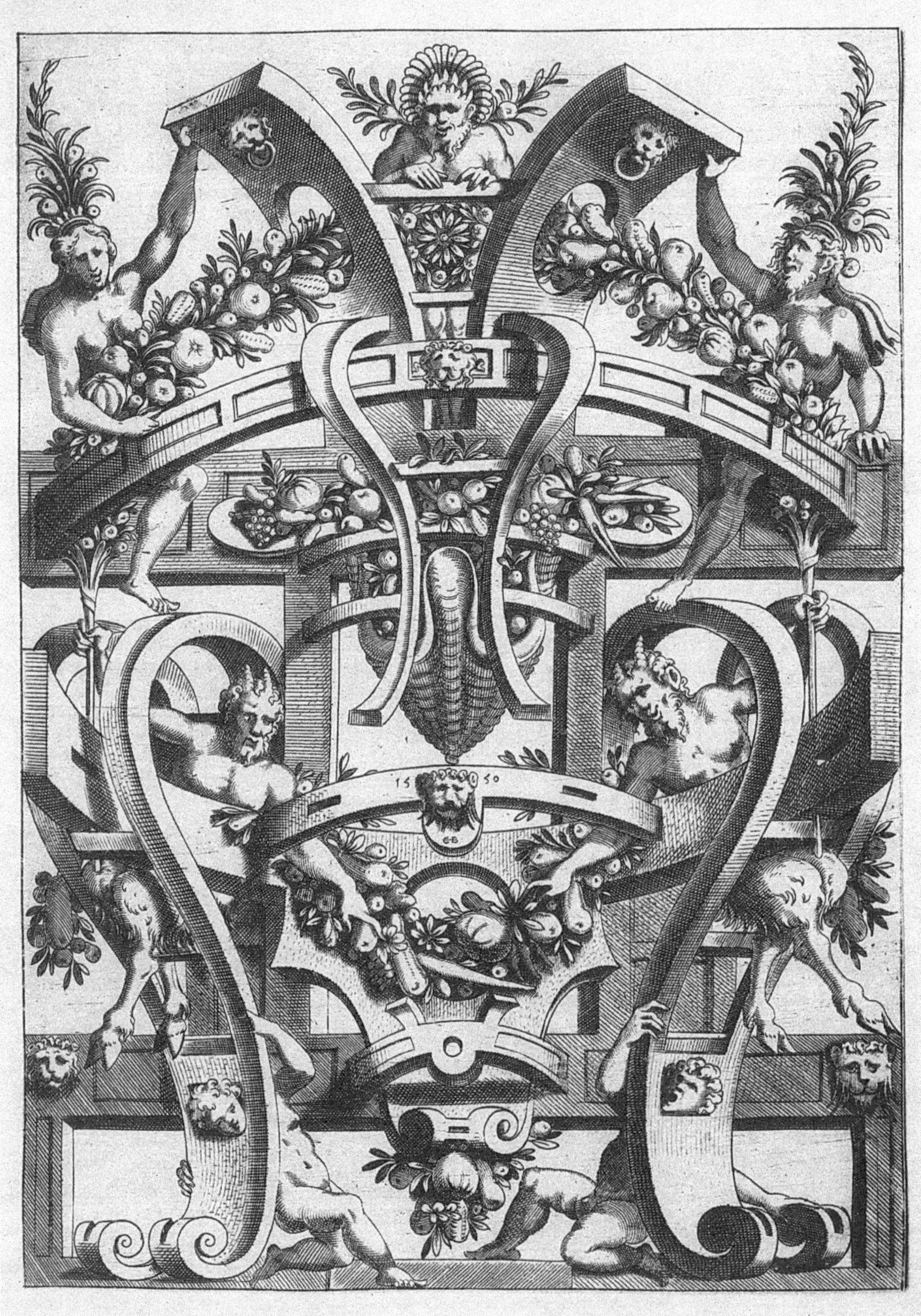

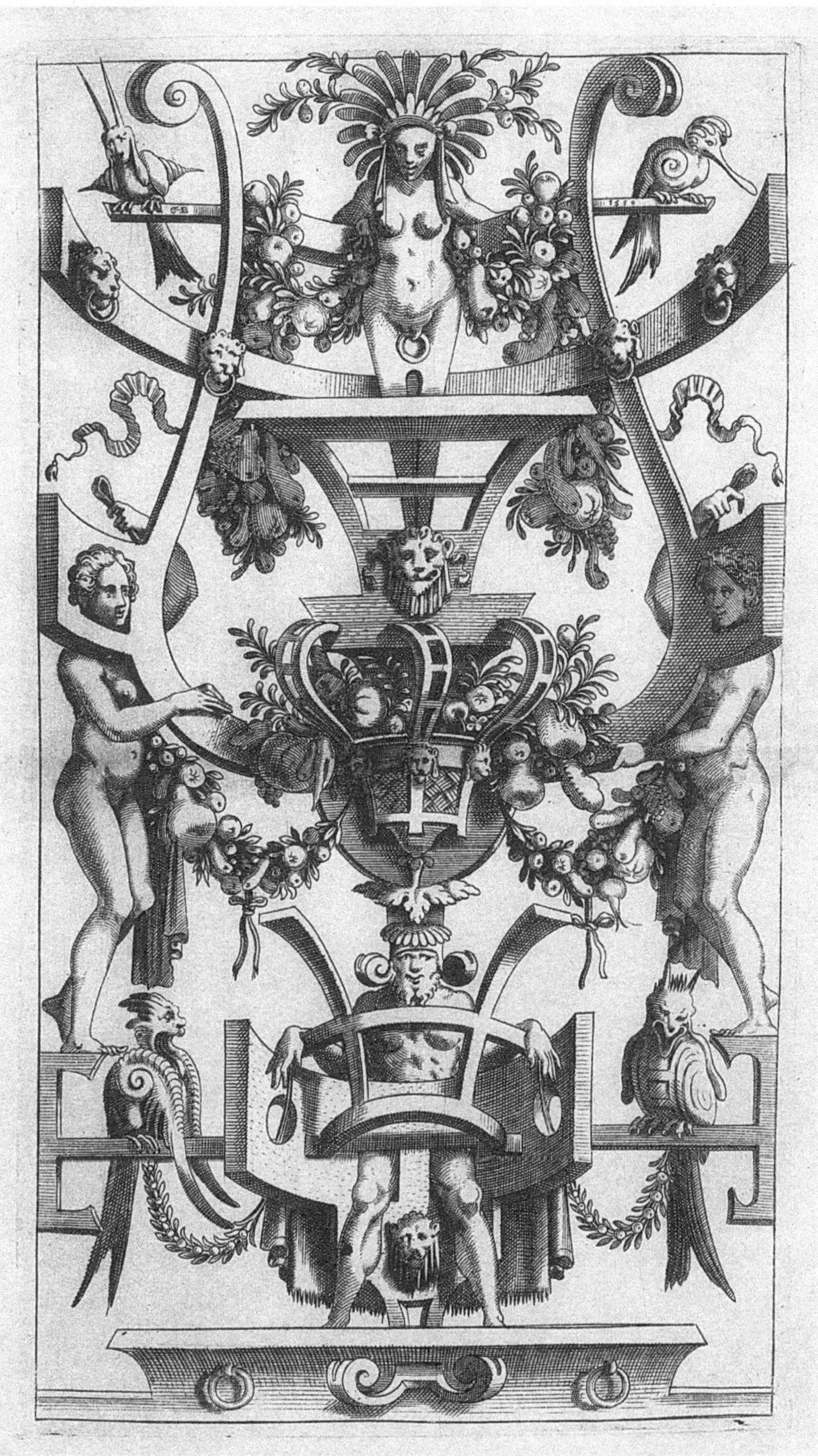

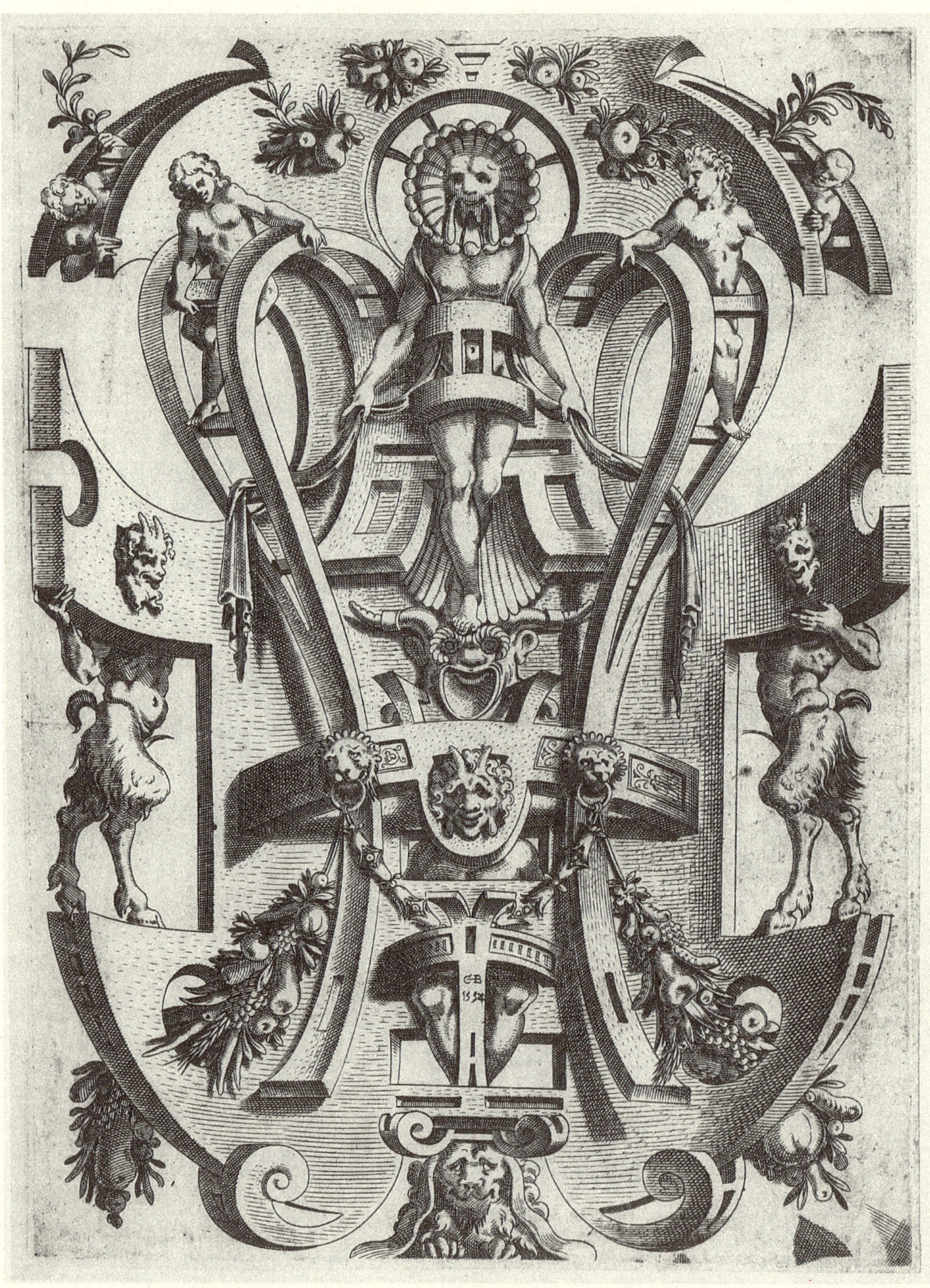

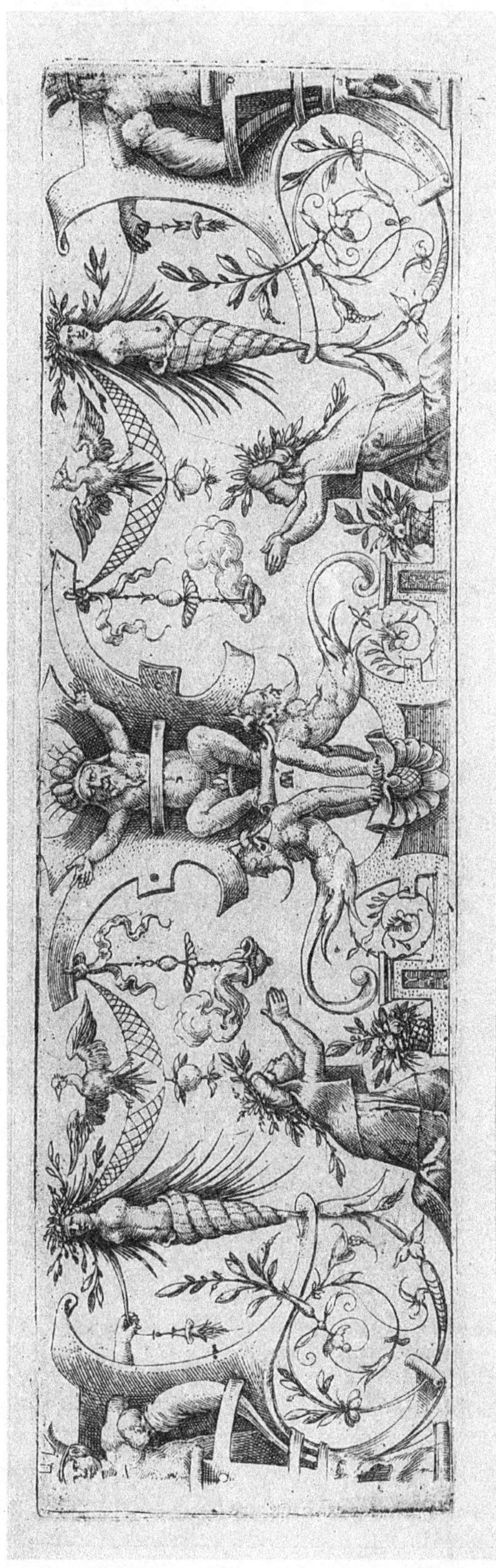

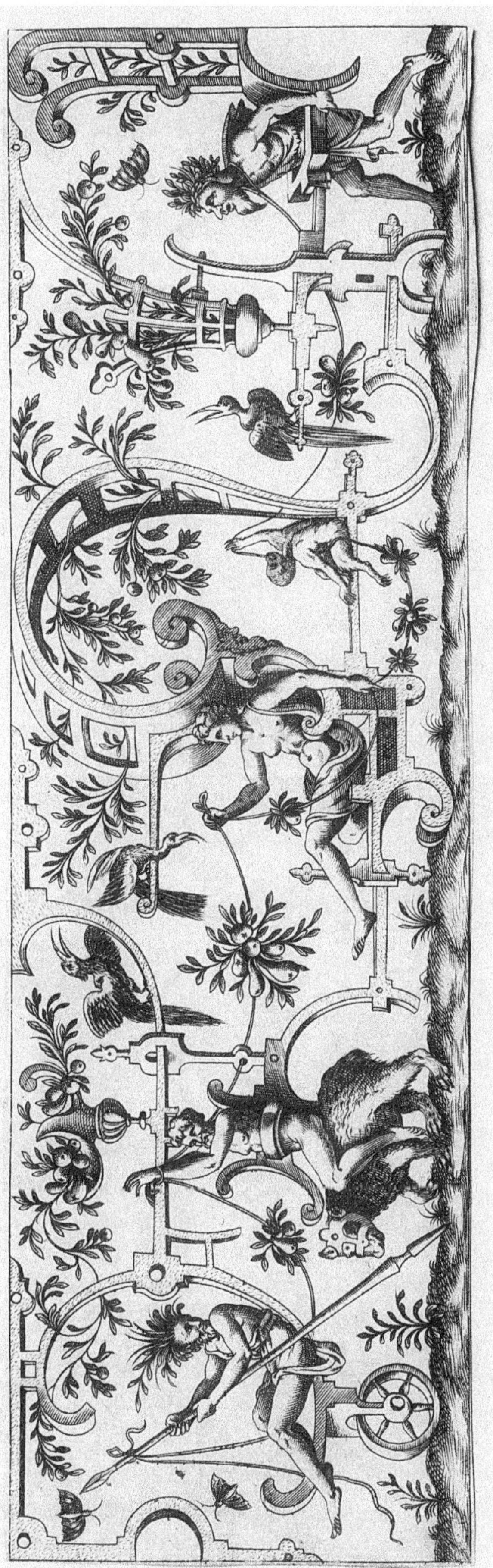

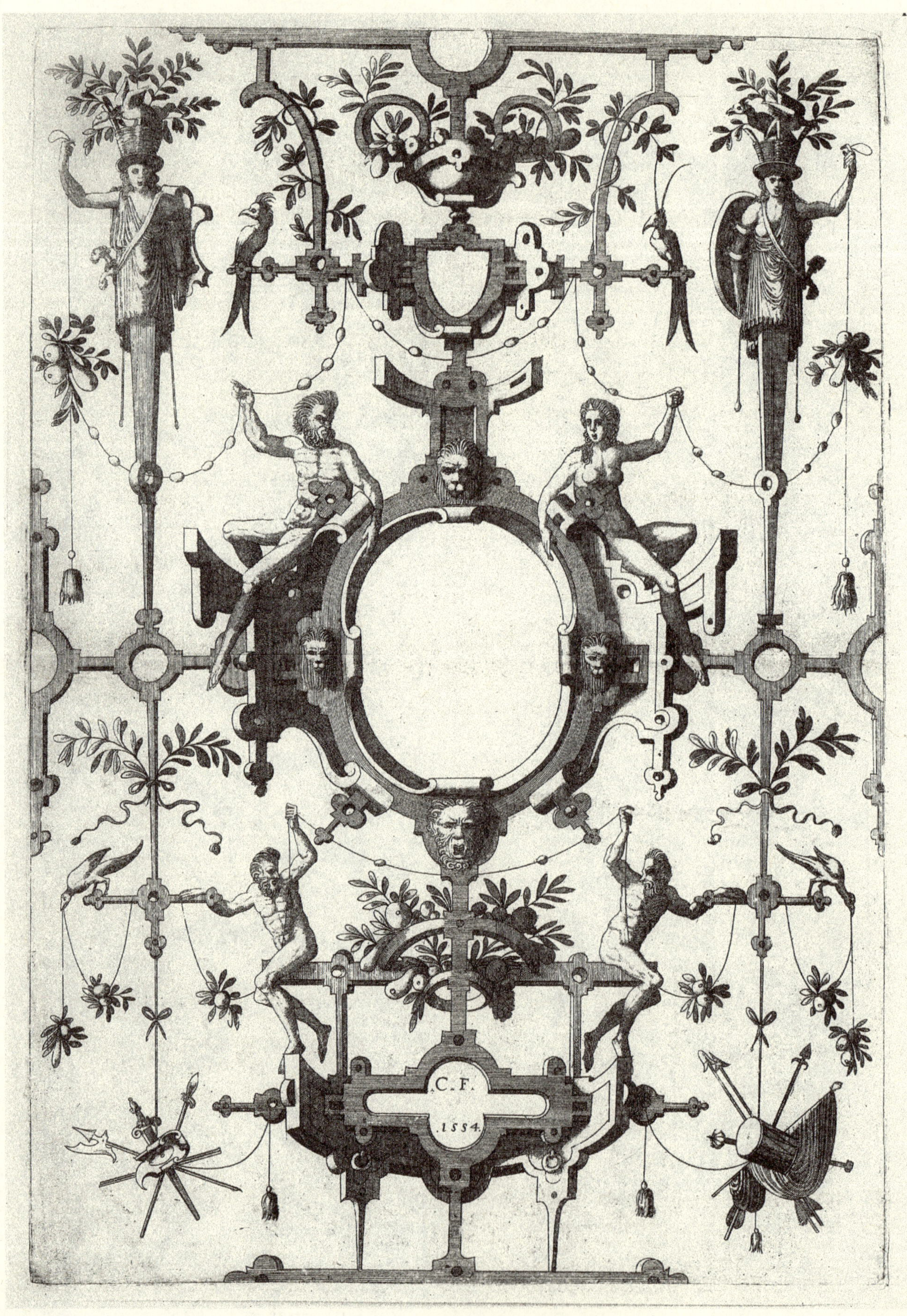

C.F.
1554.

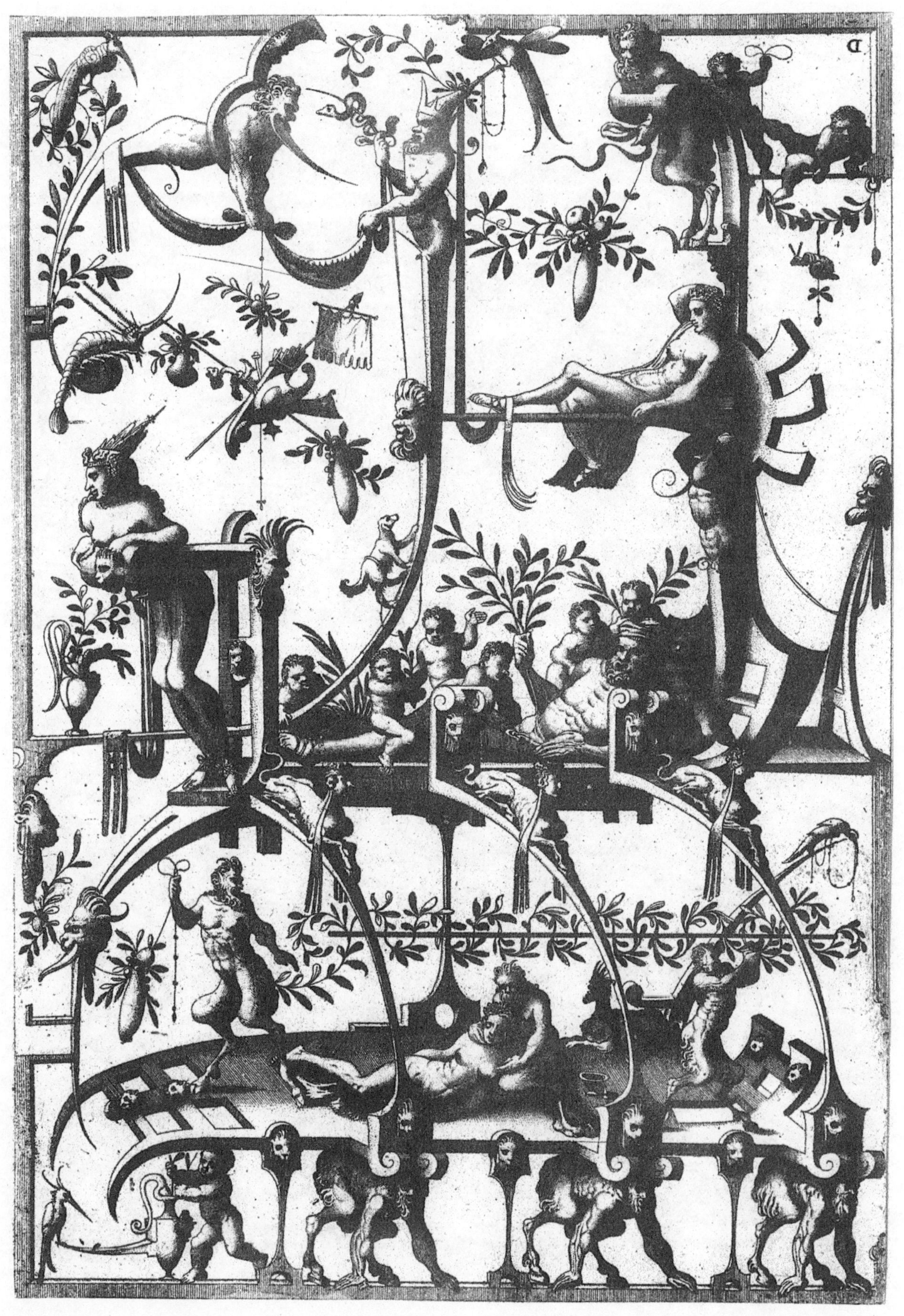

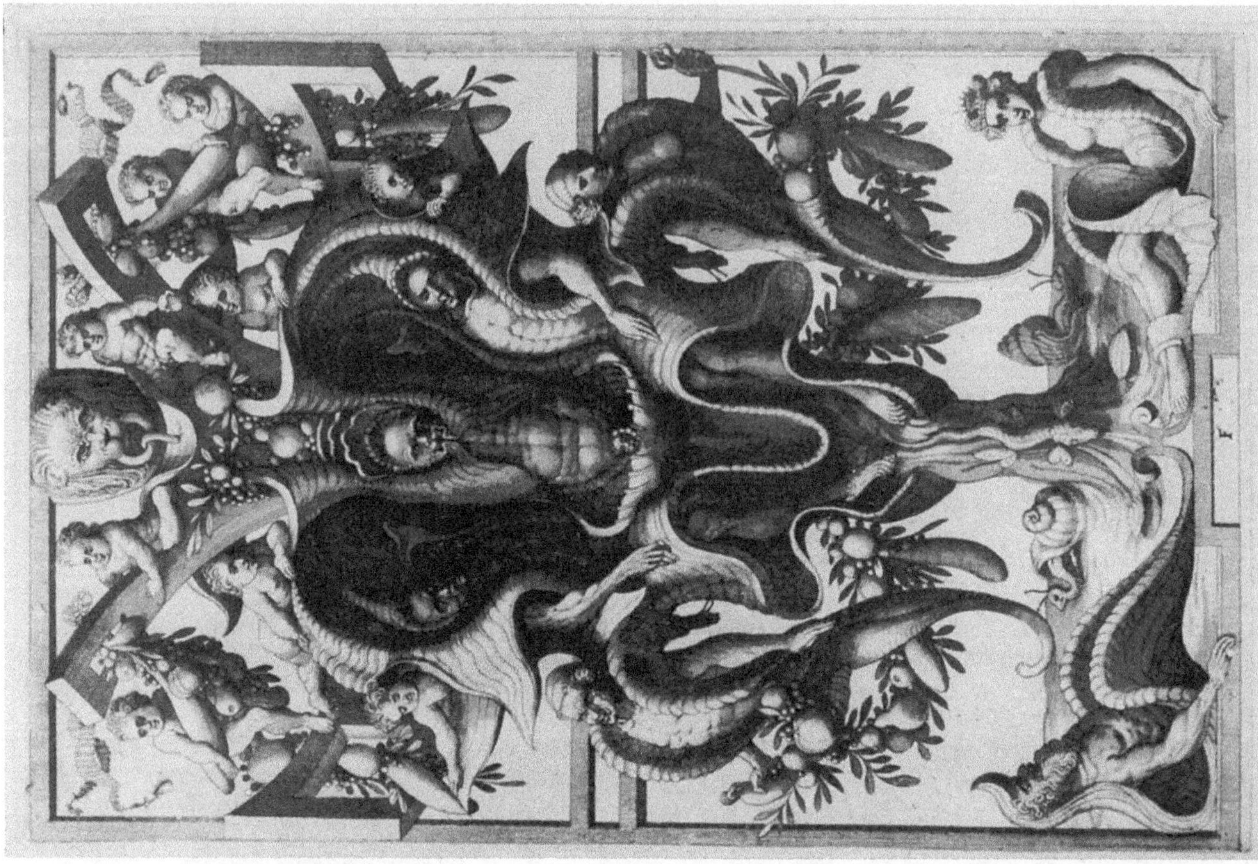

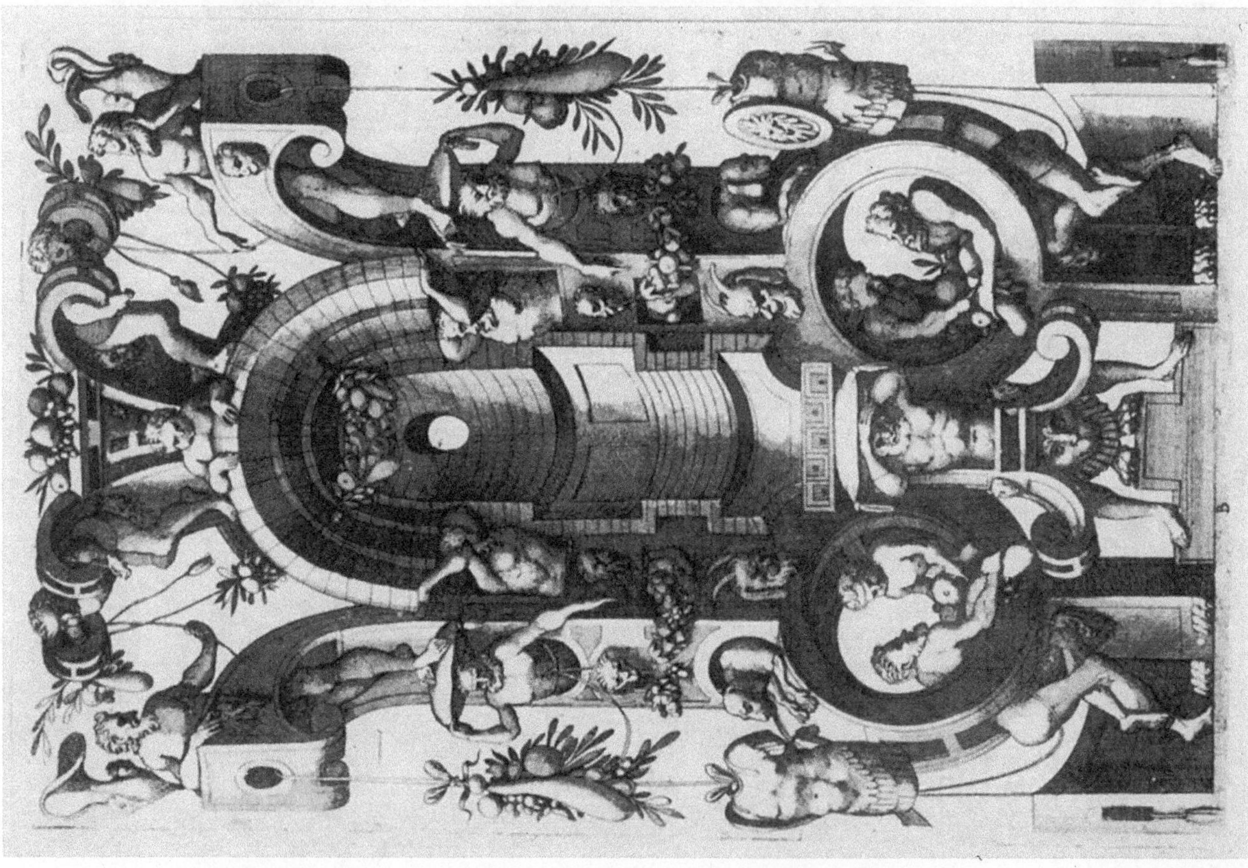

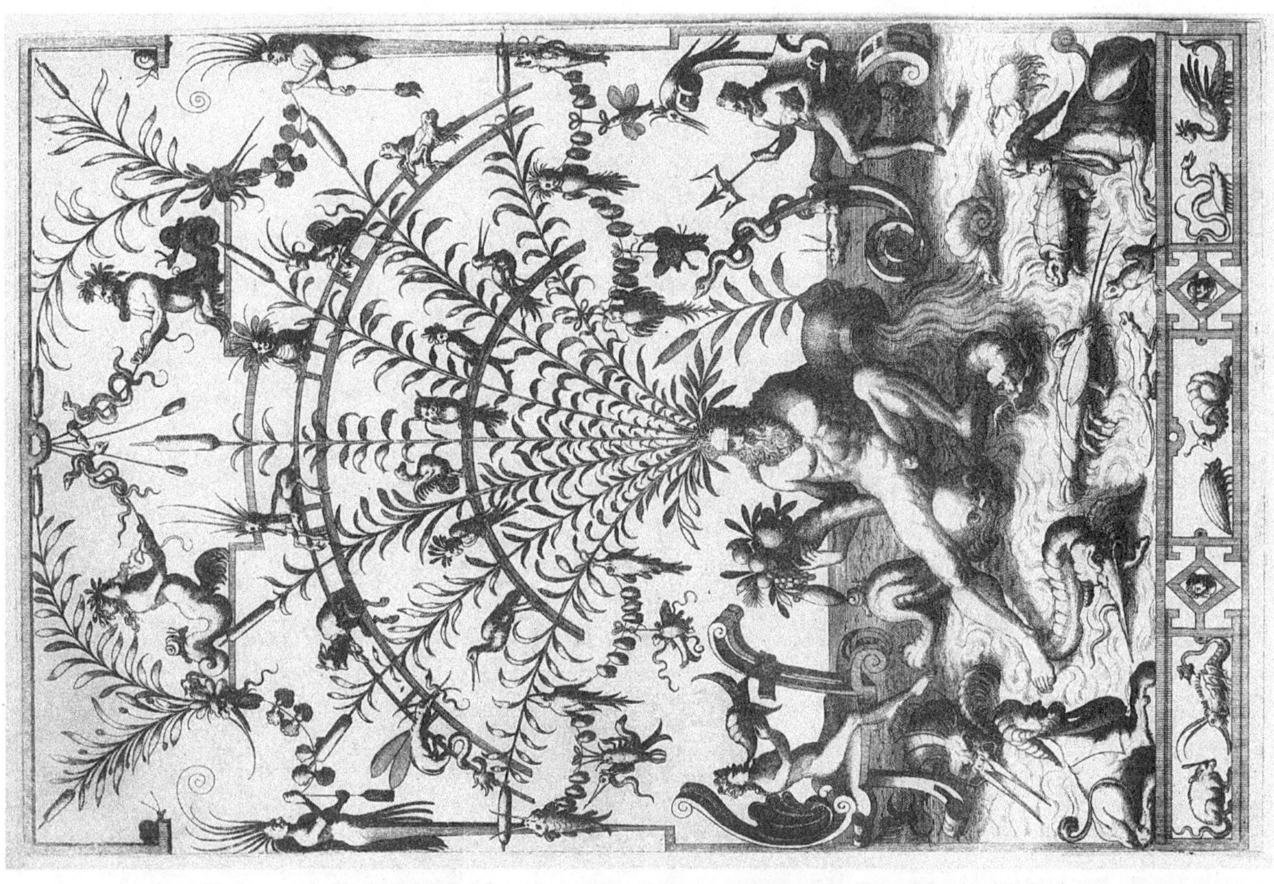

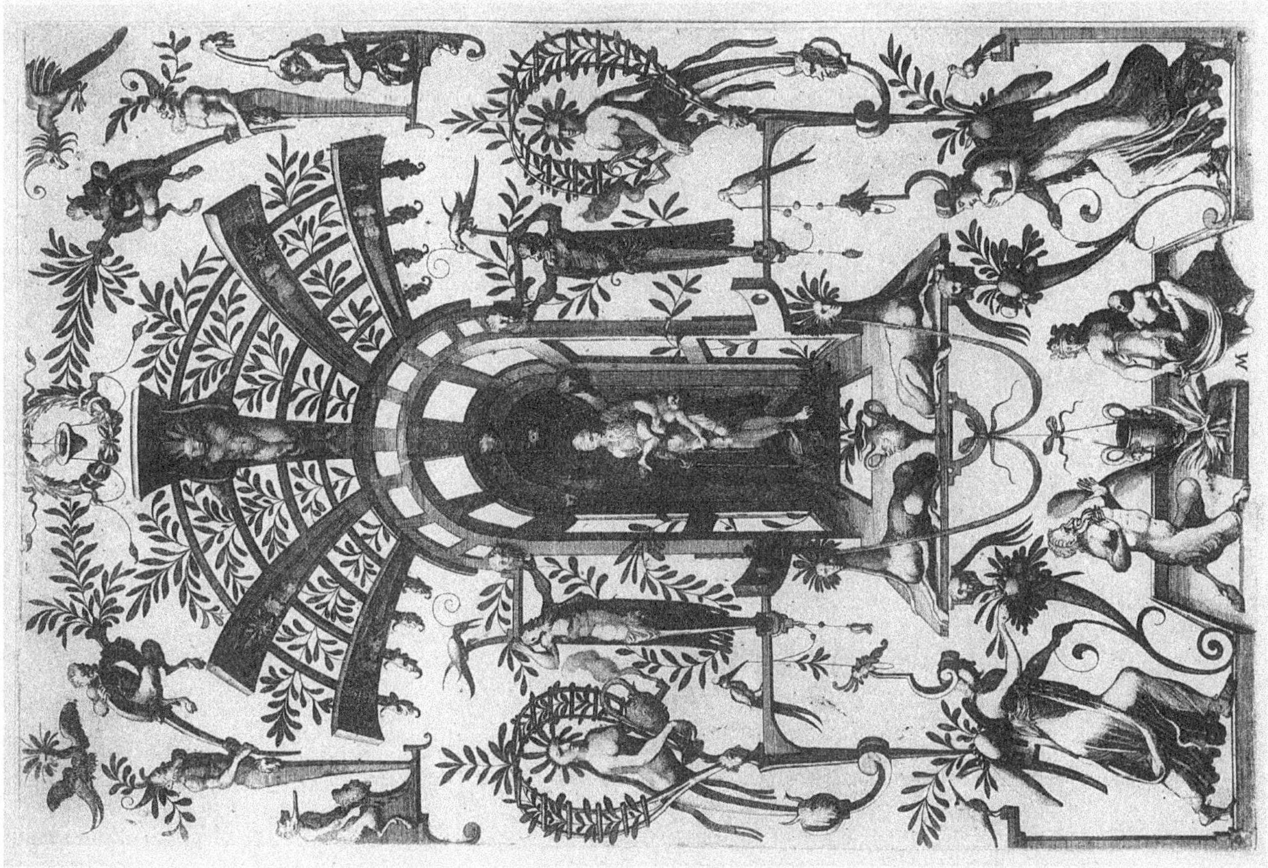

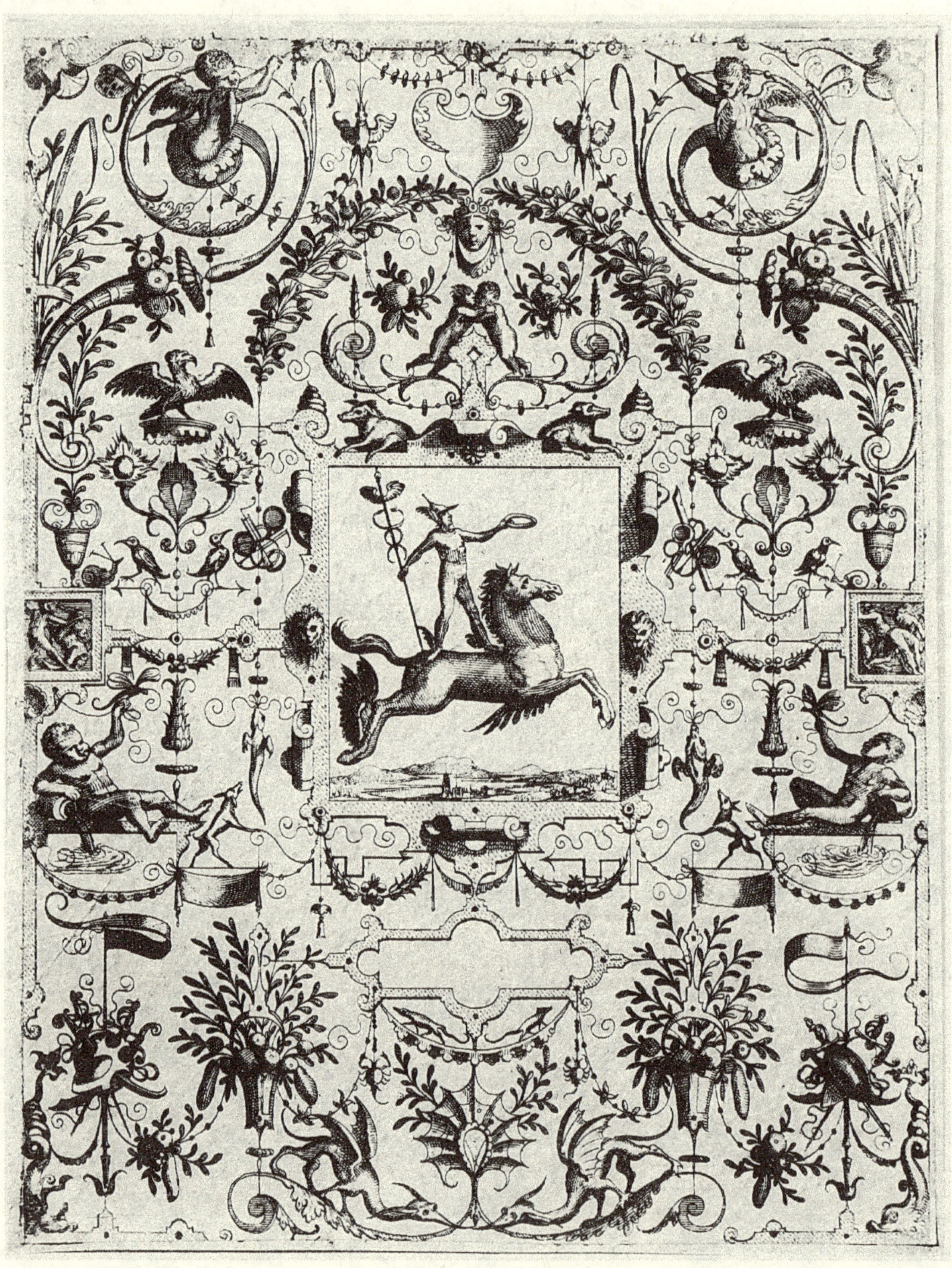

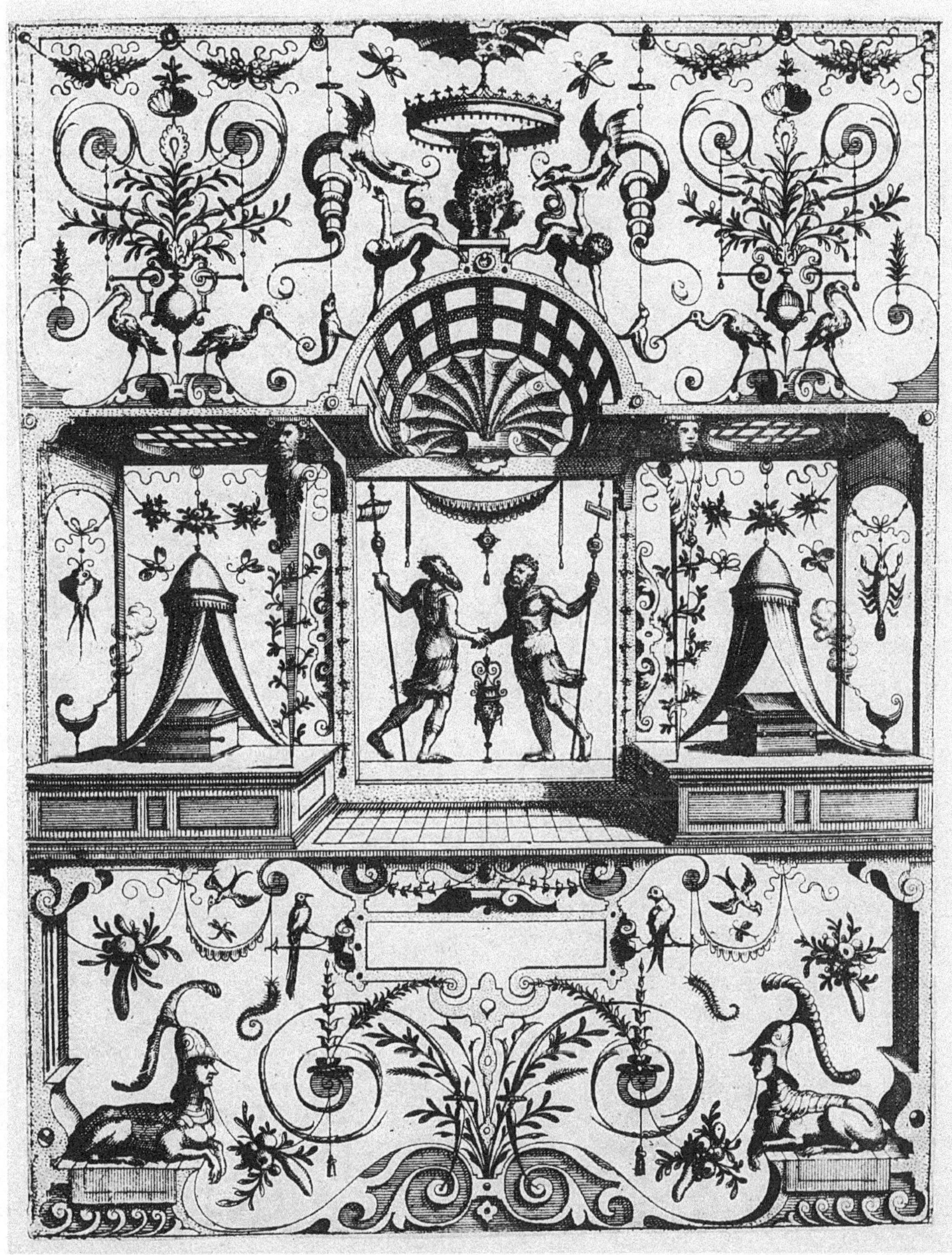

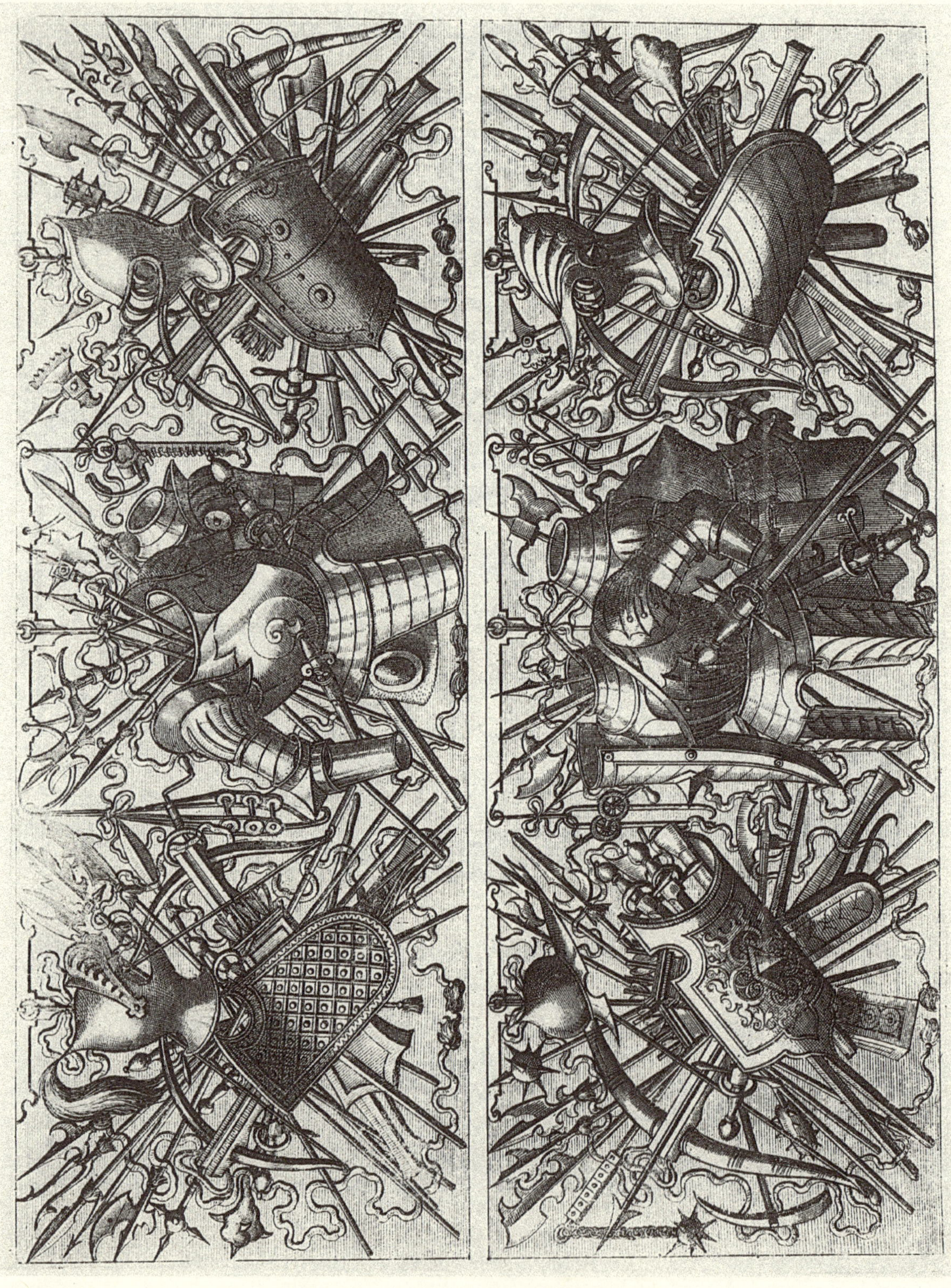

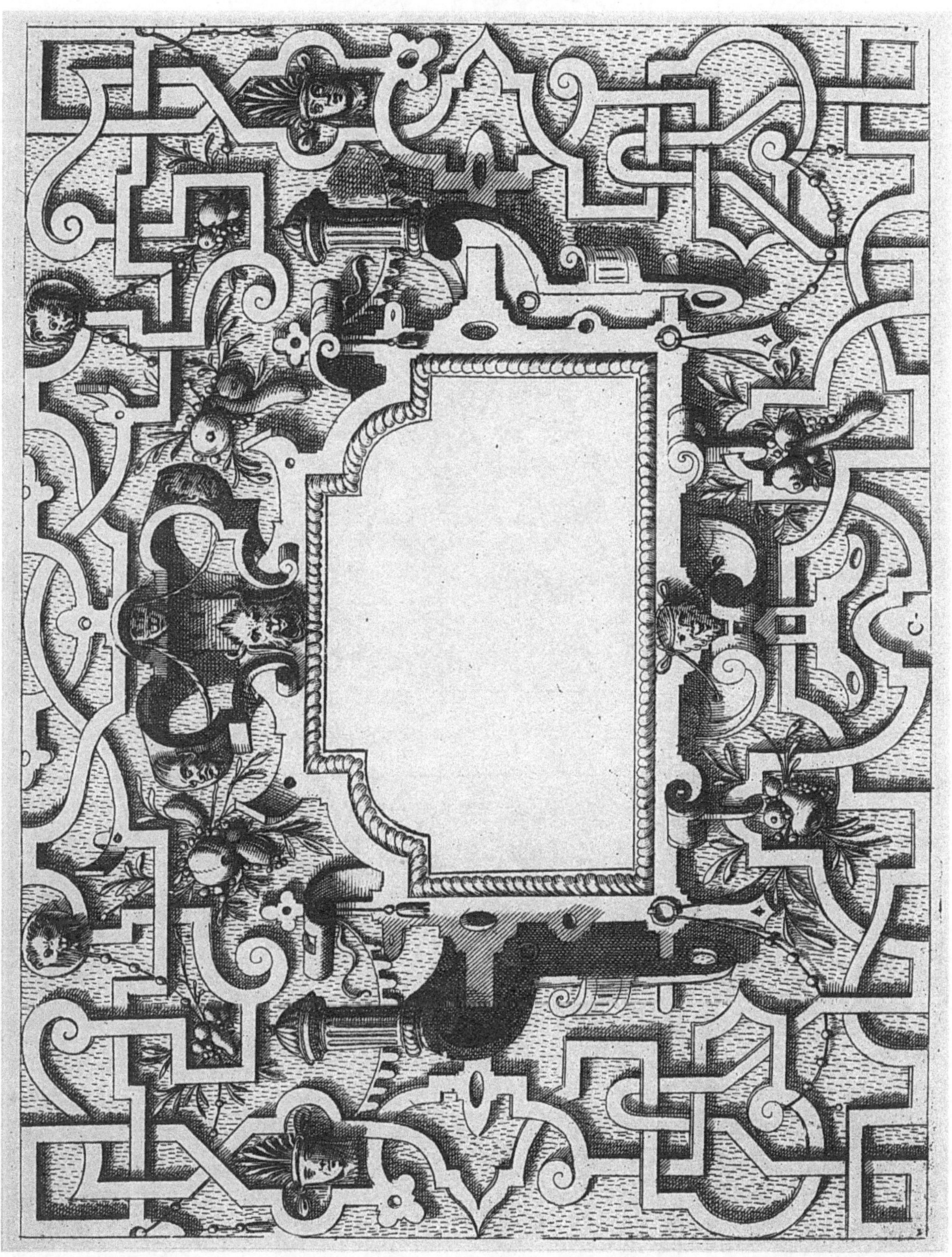

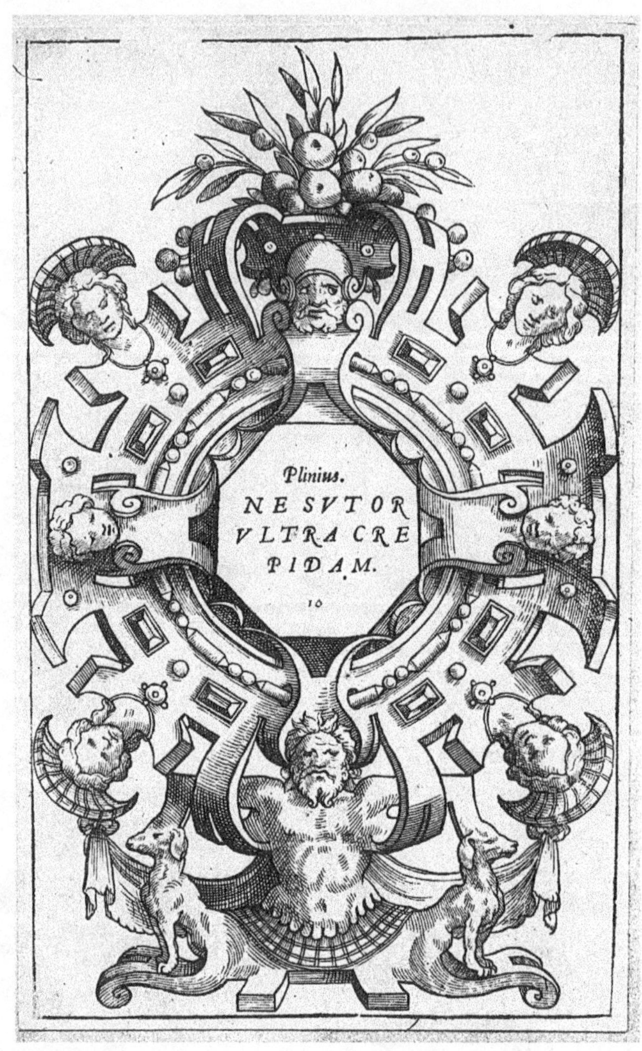
Plinius.
NE SVTOR
VLTRA CRE
PIDAM.
10

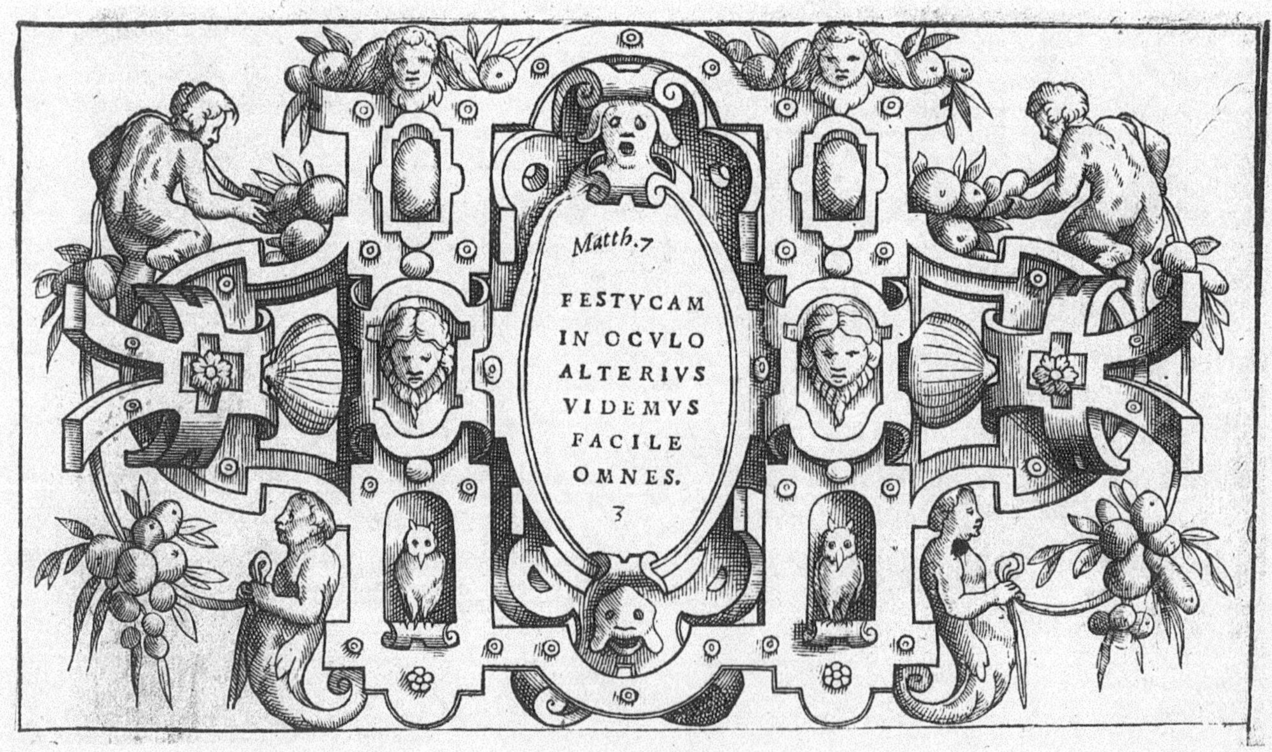
Matth.7
FESTVCAM
IN OCVLO
ALTERIVS
VIDEMVS
FACILE
OMNES.
3

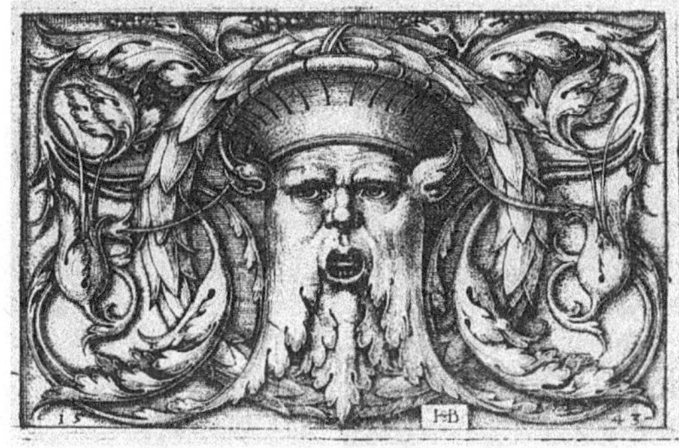
15 HSB 43

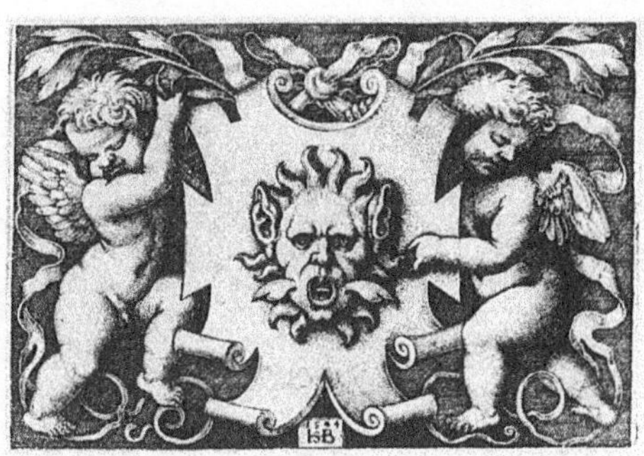

HSB

15 HSB 46

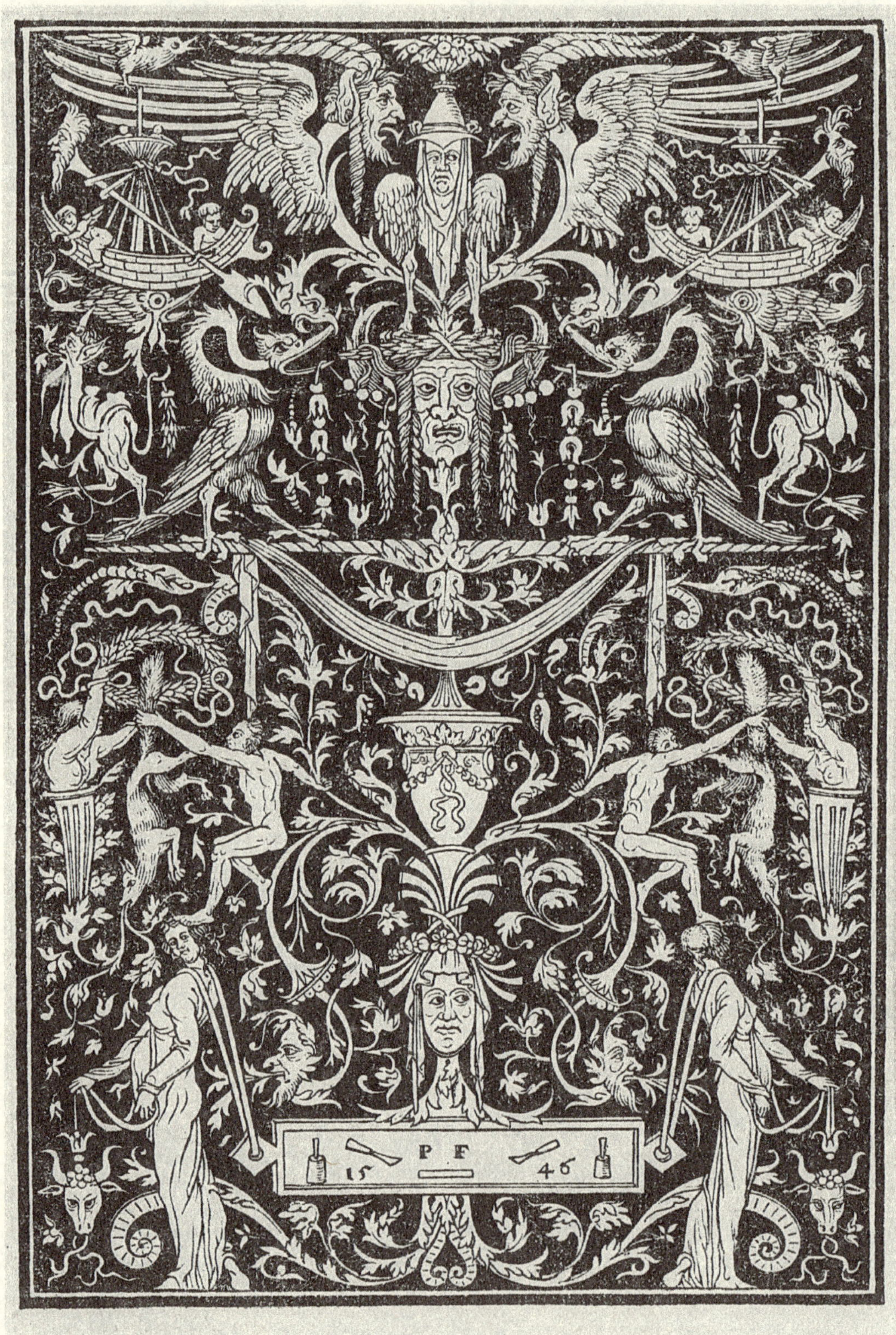
P F
15 46

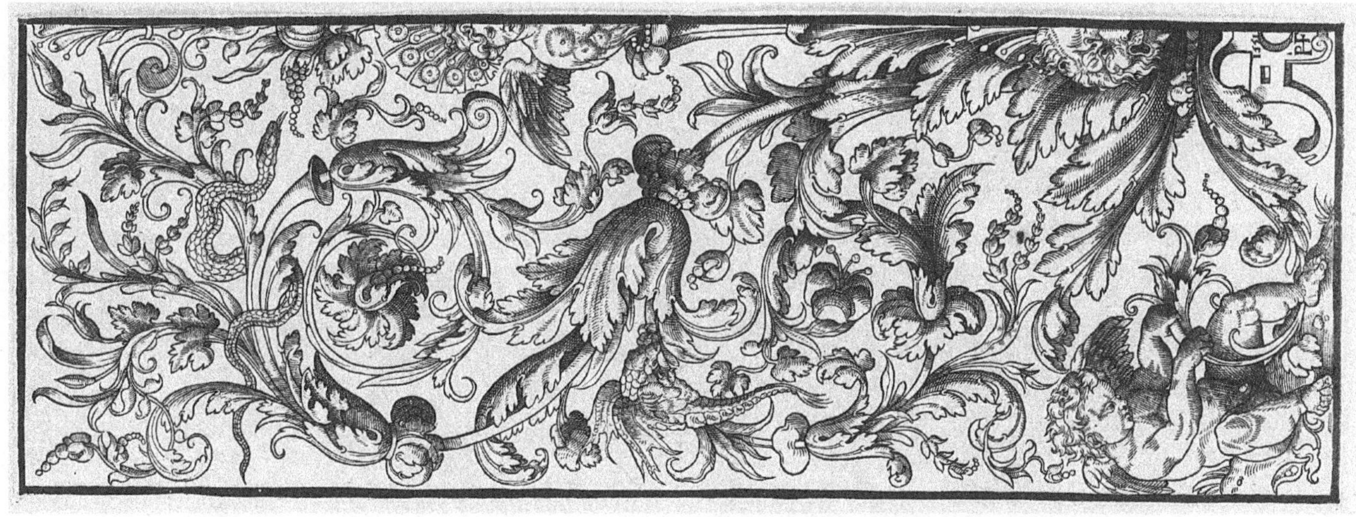

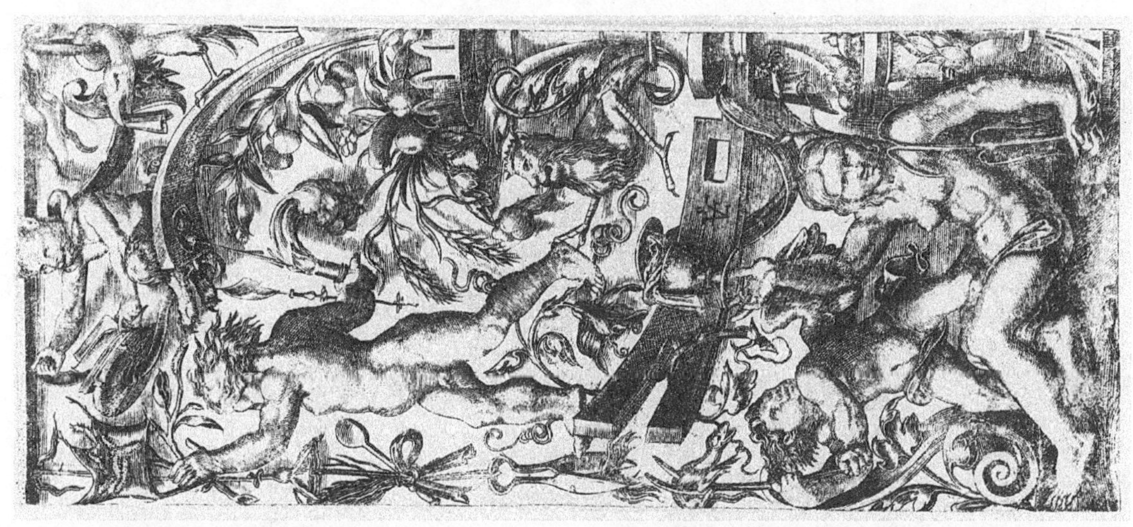

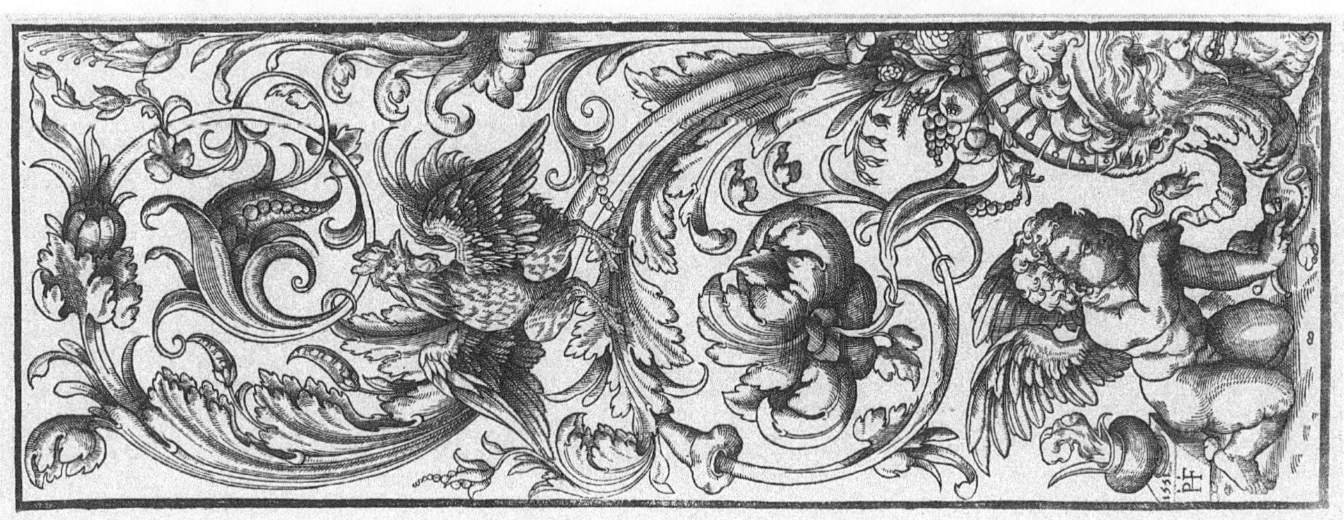

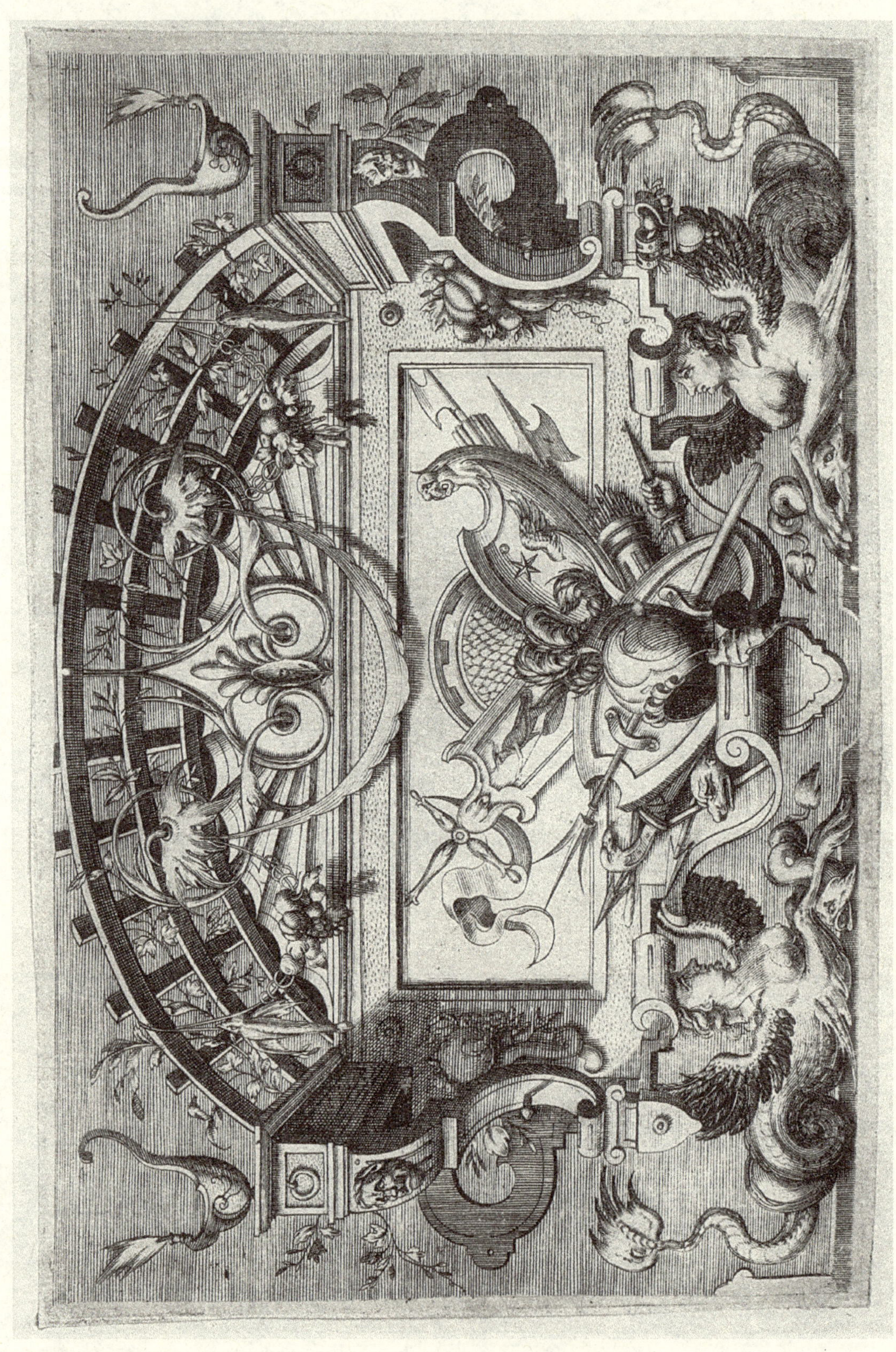

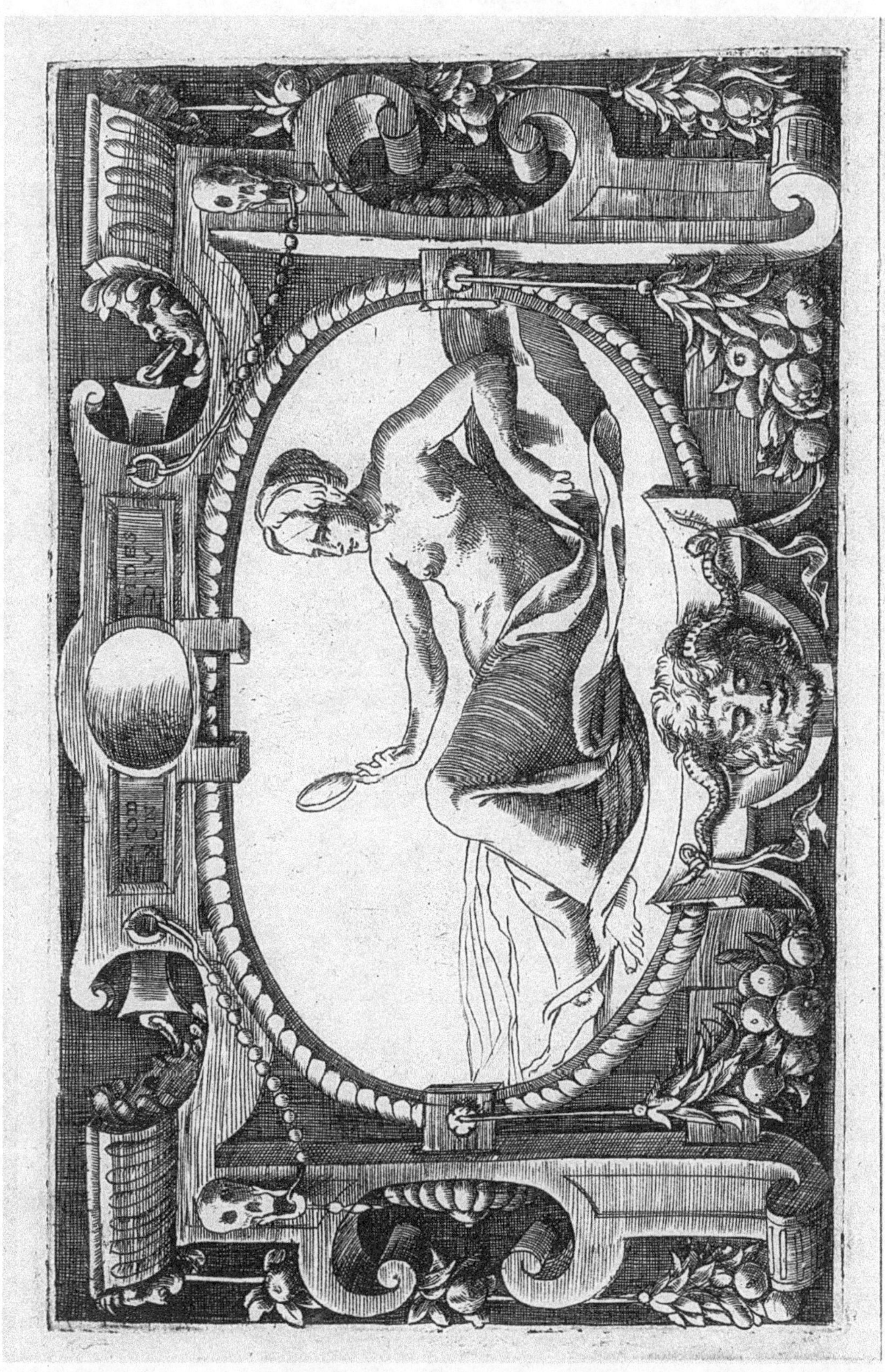

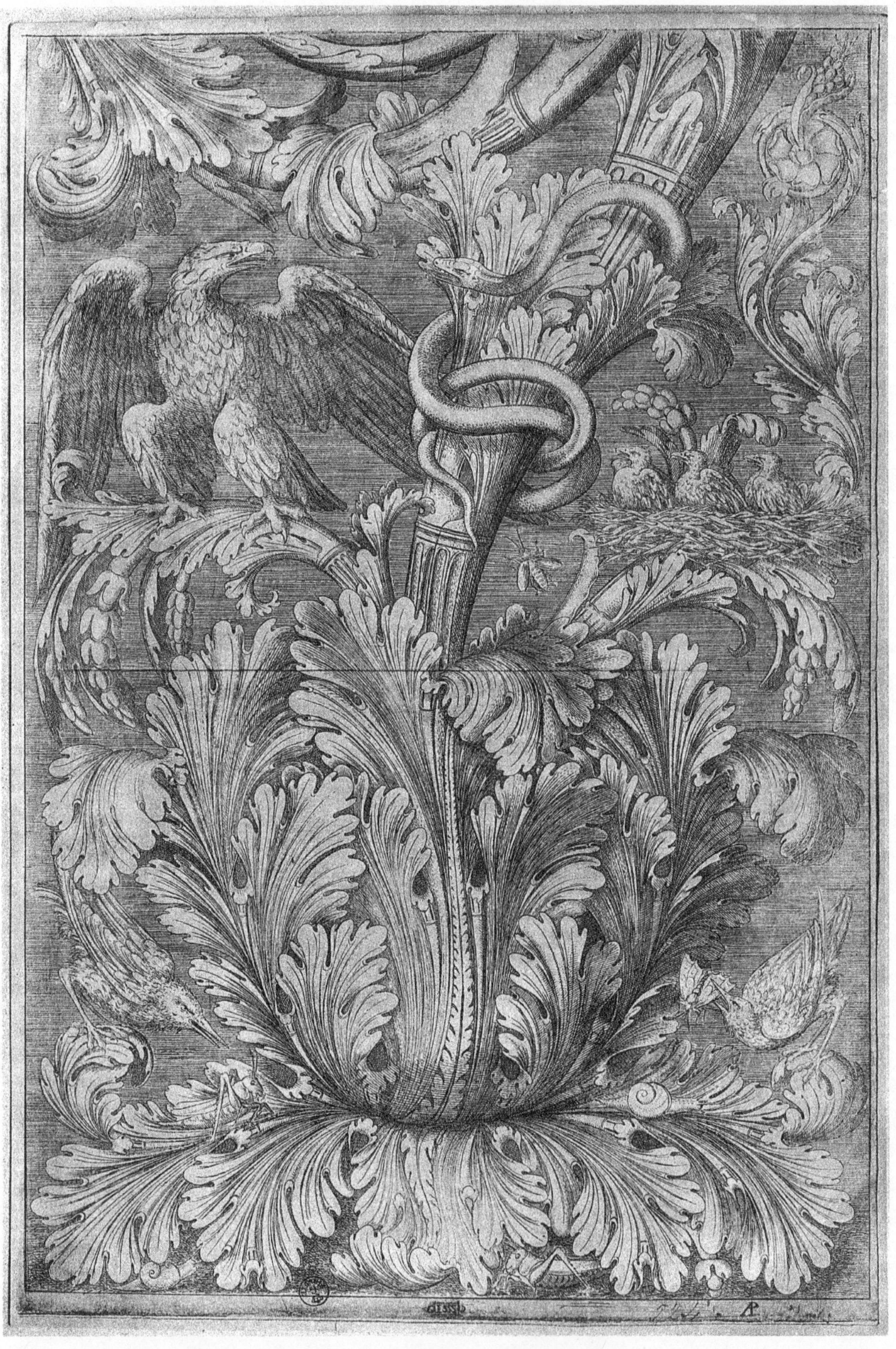

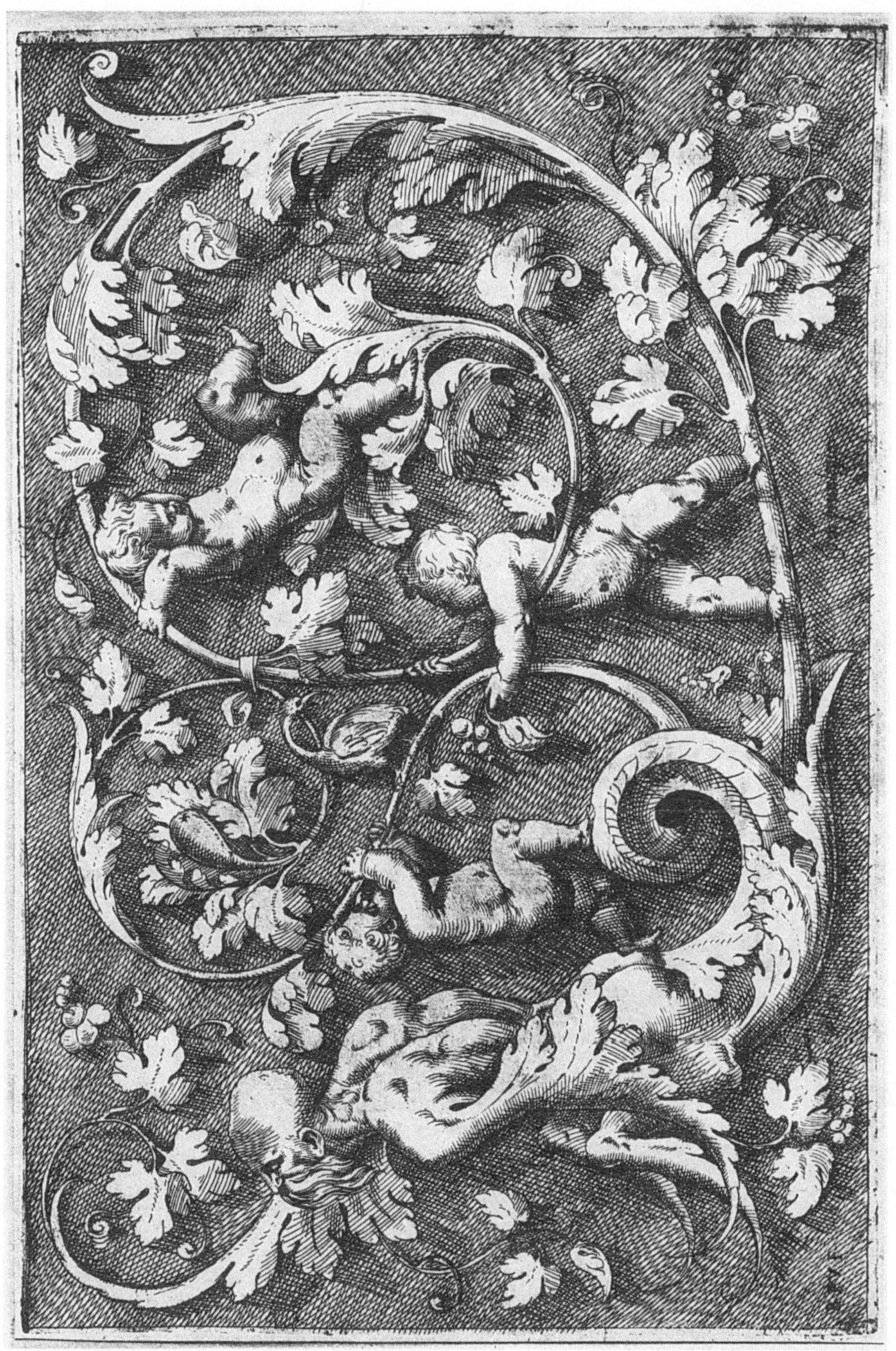

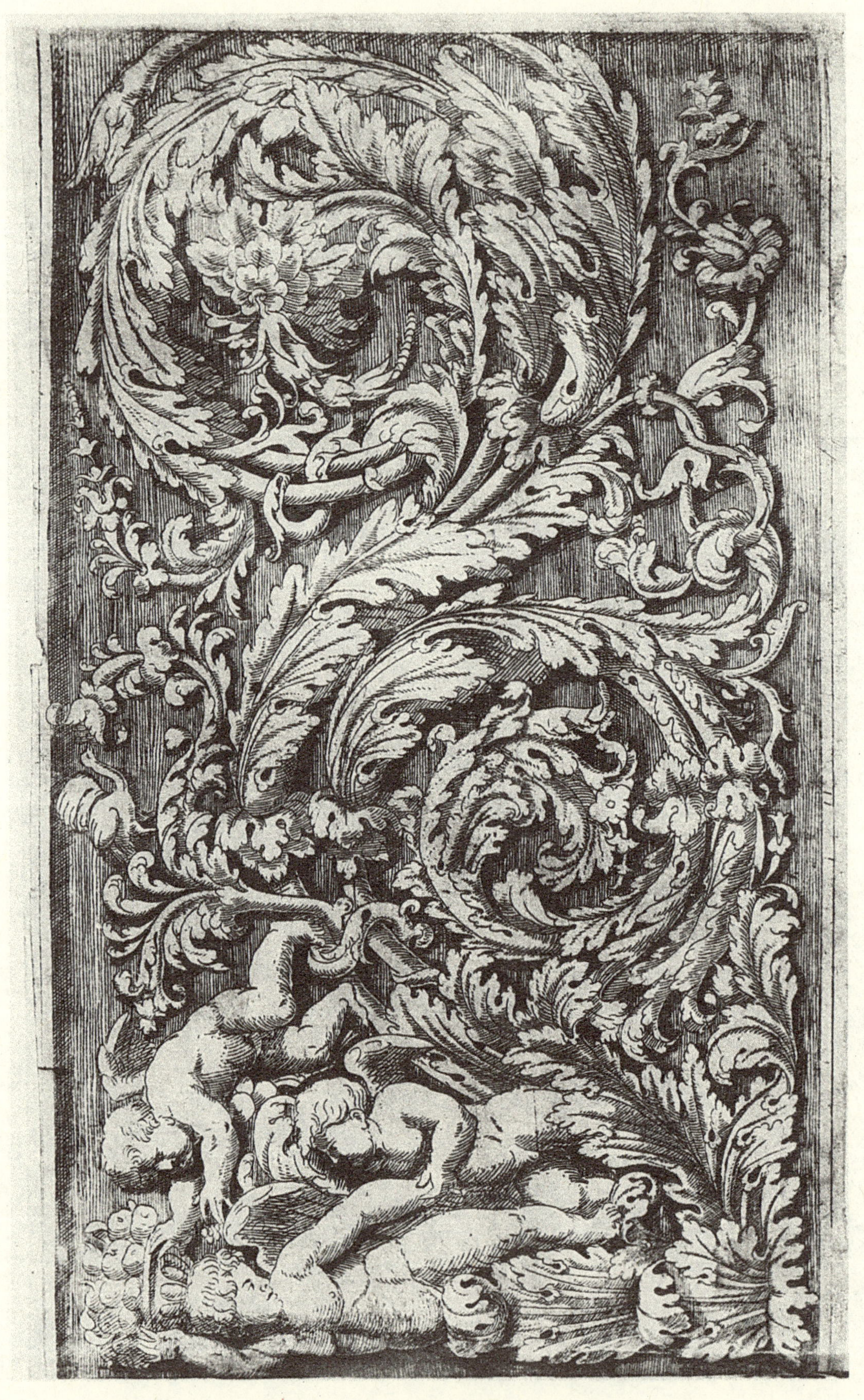

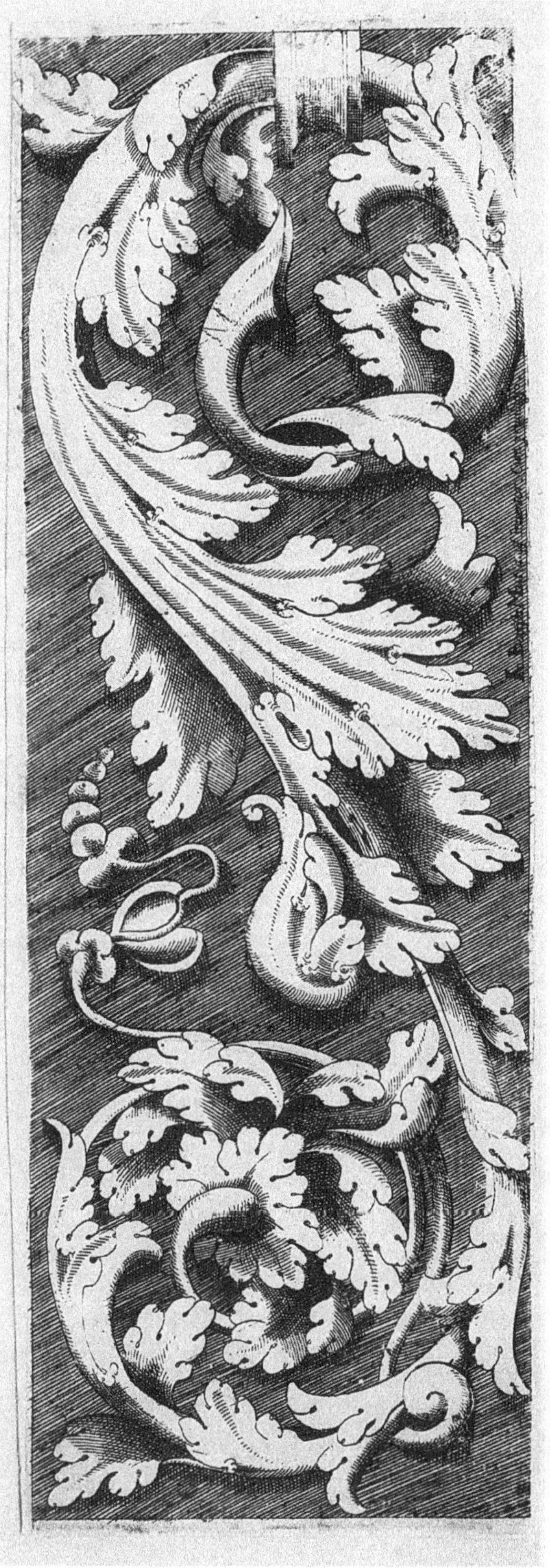

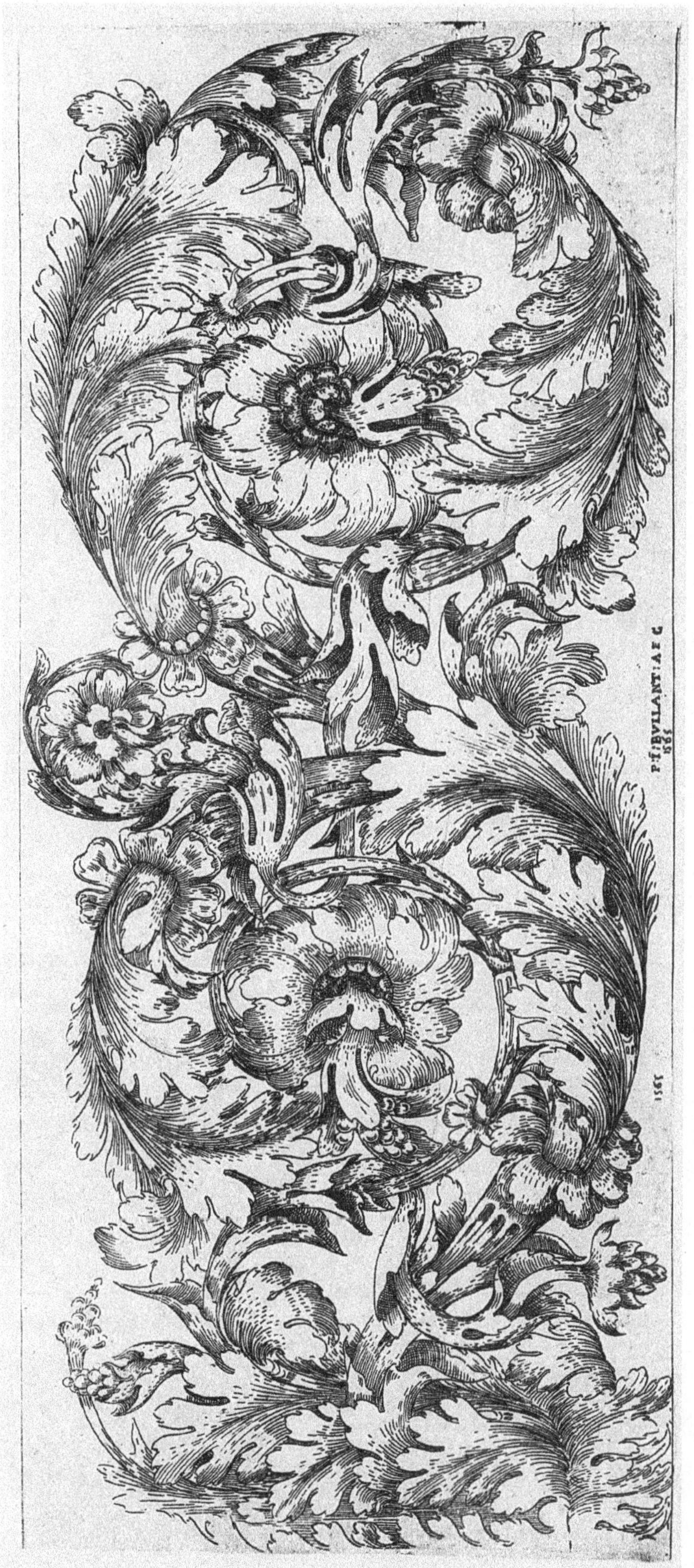

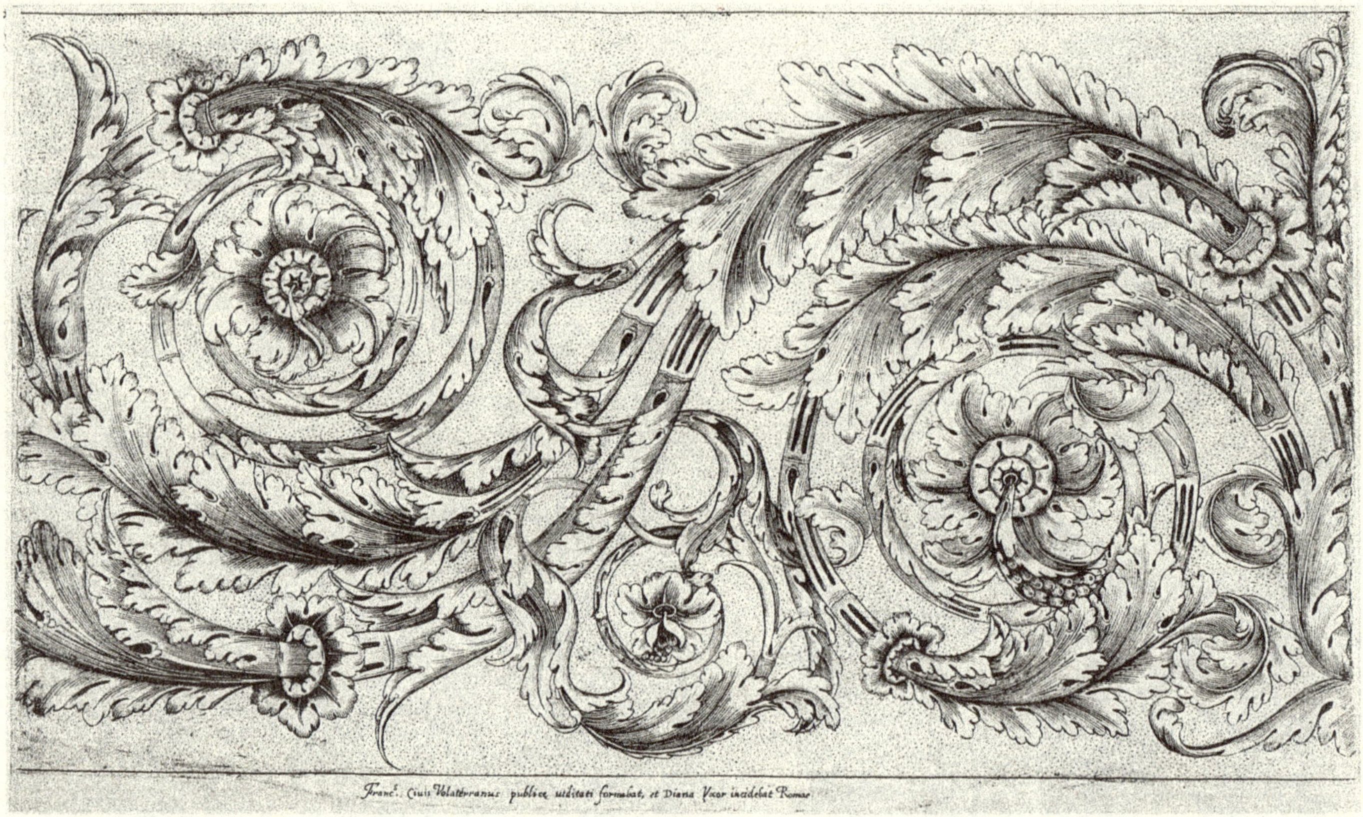

Franc^s. Ciuis Volaterranus publicę utilitati formabat, et Diana Vxor incidebat Romae

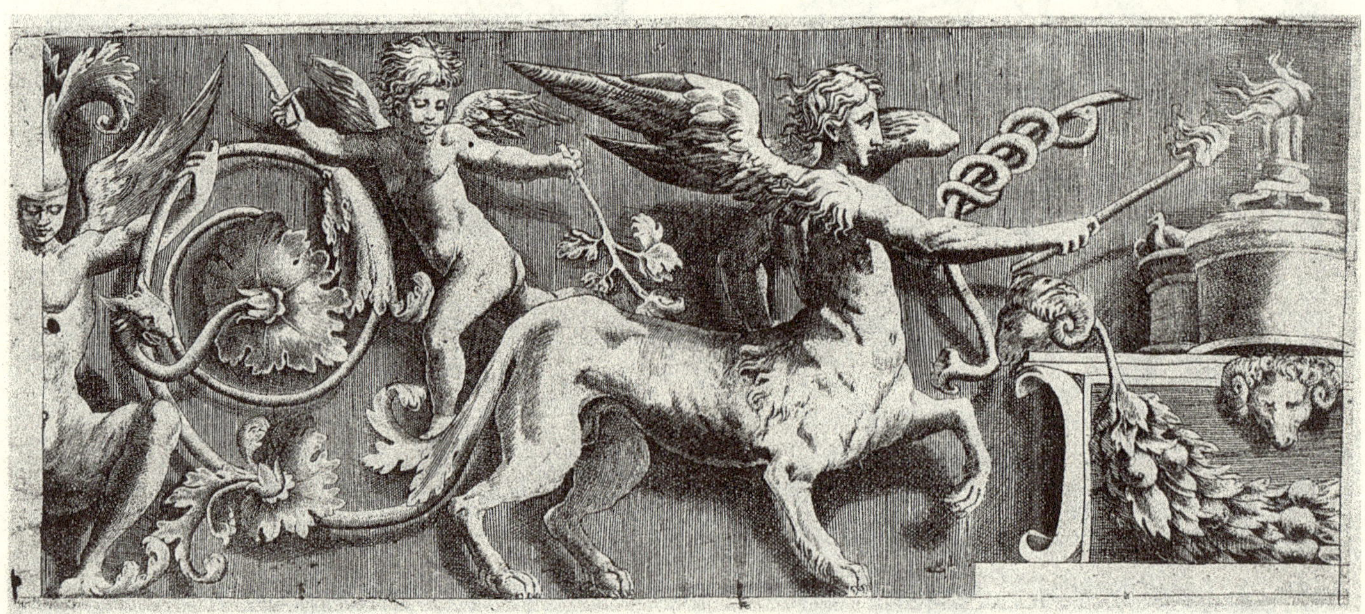

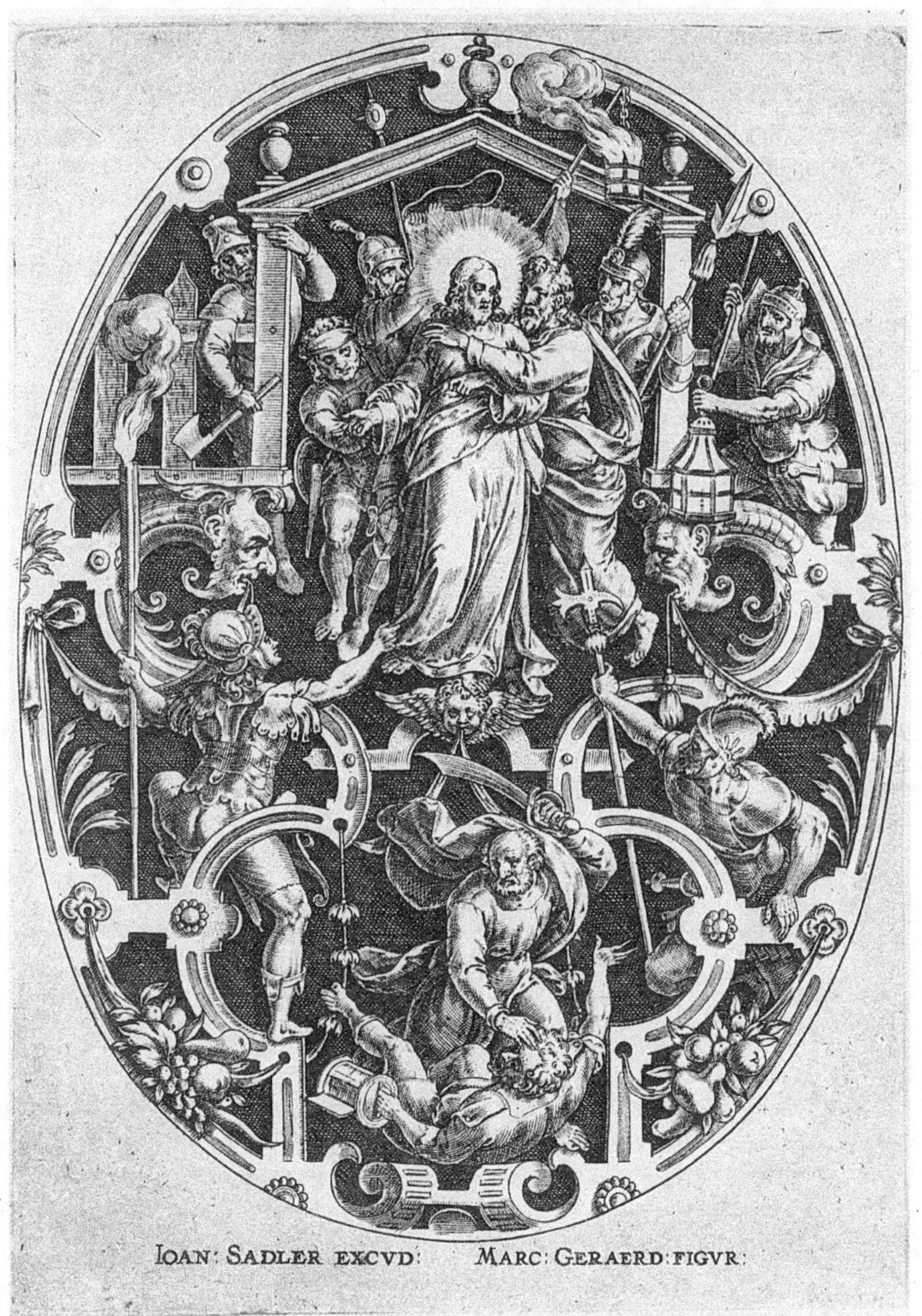
IOAN: SADLER EXCVD: MARC: GERAERD: FIGVR:

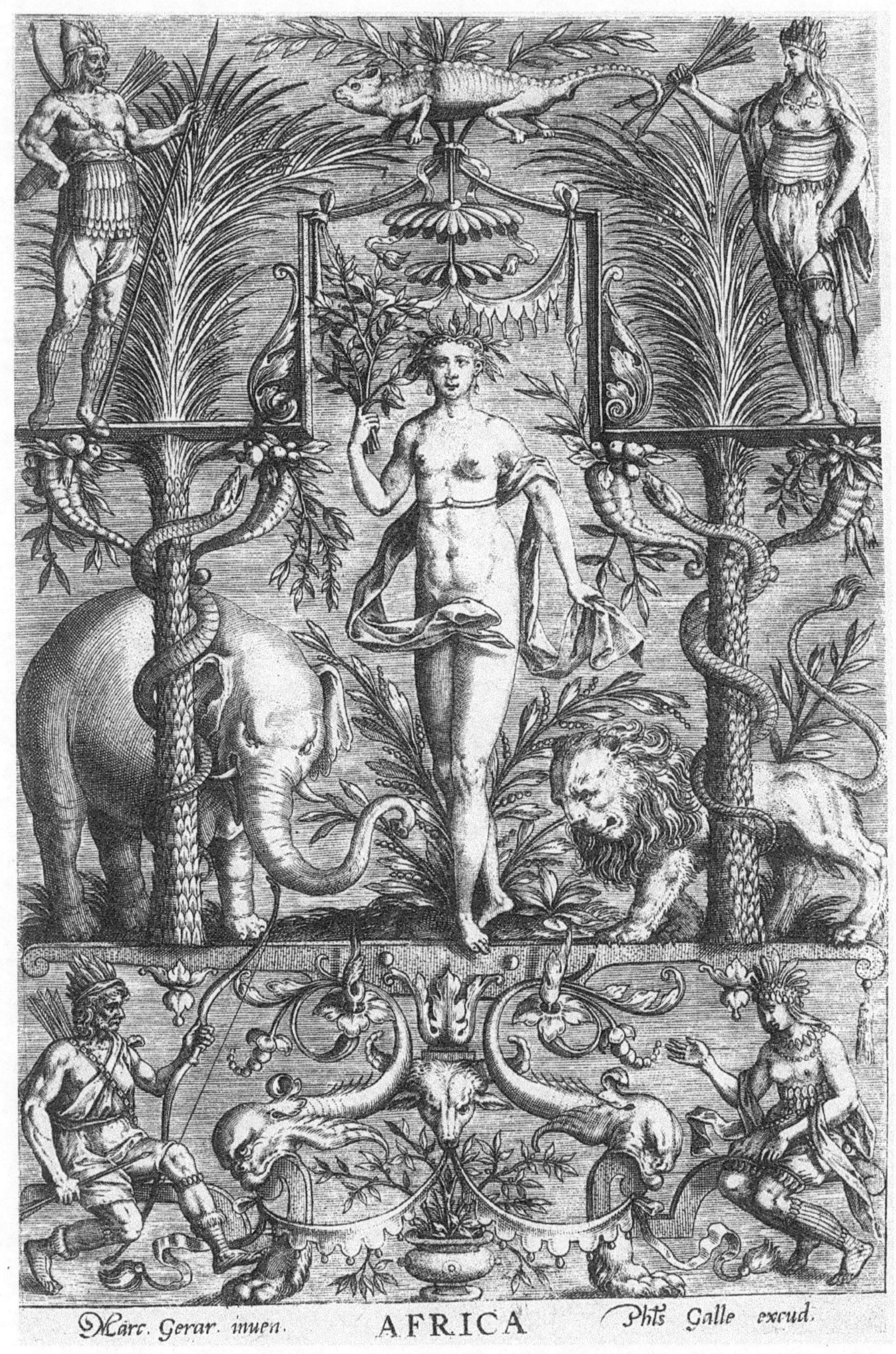
Marc. Gerar. inuen.
AFRICA
Phls Galle excud.